7 Hacks to Change

Habits in 30 days

How to remove bad habits and adopt good ones

by **Leon Lyons**

Mindset Mastership

About the Author

Leon Lyons is a senior coach at Mindset Mastership, a life coaching business based in London, England.

Mindset Mastership teaches clients how human behaviour really works. Through our teaching we have helped worldwide clients gain a better advantage, to develop themselves and achieve more from life.

For further details, see:

MindsetMastership.com

Table of Contents

What are Habits?

Habits are formed by repeating specific acts. They become stronger by the increase in the number of repeated acts. –

Mortimer J. Alder

Chapter 1

Introduction

Habits are frequently practised in repetitive behaviours. These are often subconscious behaviour patterns gained through frequent repetition. Many are unconscious because we don't even realize we're doing them.

Merriam-Webster (1928) describes habits as:

1. An acquired behaviour that has become almost or entirely accidental

2. The dominant behaviour or character of the thoughts and feelings of a person

3. A settled pattern or repetitive activity

4. A behaviour pattern developed by repetition or physiological stimulation showing itself in regularity or increased performance.

We can see that patterns characterize our personalities, our thoughts and feelings, and our' normal behaviours. We can also see that habits are activities that are almost or entirely unconscious, and we become 'better' at them because they are replicated regularly (increased performance facility).

After understanding your habits, you need to classify them ask to which are right for you and which are harmful; then you need to realise that if you want to live a healthy and prosperous life, you need to change your few bad habits? Replacing a pattern is not easy, but we will discuss some steps in this book to change your habits.

1.1 Understanding habits

We develop common ways of thinking, hearing, speaking, moving, and perceiving. This includes all our signature behaviours, emotions, vocal habits, facial expressions, and mannerisms. Mental practices help us organize the experience, and our motor patterns make it possible to act quickly and automatically.

Consequently, a habit has positive value as a structure that allows us to cope with reality as it presents itself. It can have distinct drawbacks on the other hand. The propensity to rely on our usual ways of behaving and reacting can blind us to the novel and unusual, comfort us into seamlessness, prevent us from adapting to change, and deceive us into applying old solutions to new issues. Habits tend to work on an unconscious, automatic level. Generally, we don't know we're developing them, and we don't even realize we're using them. The golfer can rarely tell when he started to slice and may fail to recognise that as he swings, the ball spins. In every other sentence, the speaker who says, "as it was" has no idea that he does so until his wife points it out. In the psychology of perception, some of the most startling examples of unconscious action are found. The cues we use to see distance - perspective, colour, and variations in brightness - are so natural that we don't know we're using them.

How rigid are our perceptual habits? In response to this question, Stratton (1897) conducted a classic experiment in which he had subjects wear special lenses reversing the field of vision, both left and right and above and below. Surprisingly, it took the subjects only a few days to modify their deeply rooted habits, and they got used to be seeing down as up, and things that appeared on the right reached to the left.

Another experimenter, Foley (1940), not only distorted an adult monkey's visual field in these two ways but also made him see as far and as close as possible. The monkey reached, climbed, and walked practically within eight days. It took him three days to adjust when the lenses were removed revealing the standard perceptual field.

Willey et al. (1937) conducted a similar experiment with hearing using a device called a pseudo-phone. His human subjects wore earphones that transmitted sounds to the left ear from the right side, and vice versa. At first, this created confusion, but again the participants soon learned to adapt to the new conditions. These tests show that some of our most simple behaviours can be changed - a good thing to remember when you are called upon to adapt to new circumstances. The recruit may never like the food from the army, but he gets used to it, at least to some degree.

The person who uses a microscope for the first time is sure that he will not see anything more of a blur, but within a week or so, he begins to develop different viewing patterns that open up a new world of knowledge. The same thing occurs with the medical student as he slowly learns what to listen to when using a stethoscope.

The effect of early habit formation on the growth of the child's personality has been amply demonstrated by clinical research. Childhood disruptions can often be traced back to the time when the child acquired behavioural patterns associated with sleeping, weaning, speech, and elimination. It is now generally agreed that the parents' behaviour and the home environment are critical when teaching takes place. Encouragement, acceptance, and confidence not only promote the child's acquisition of good physical behaviours but also contribute to the development of healthy emotional patterns.

As pressure and reproof create anxiety or frustration, eventually they corrode relationships with oneself and others. Although both healthy and unhealthy habits tend to be permanent, it is crucial to recognize a curious persistence of neurotic tendencies. This is shown by the fact that when a person develops anxiety reactions in his adult life, he tends to go back to earlier habits that laid the foundation for this reaction. As a result, it set in a vicious cycle. Some of the latest behavioural therapies, such as the technique of J. Wolpe, (1990) are aimed at breaking these habits and creating new ones.

Some researchers view the process of learning in terms of habit-forming as it establishes a connection between a stimulus and a response that did not exist before. Verbal habits are a clear example: we learn to link to an instrument containing ink with the 'pen' response.

Theoretically, all other behaviours involving habit forming, such as the ability to ride a bicycle or the development of emotional reactions and attitudes, can also be viewed as learning appropriate responses to simple or complex stimuli.

Opponents of this view claim that learning is a mechanical process that lacks the role of cognitive processes. The 'cognitive' camp attempts to show that new, unexpected perspectives can be obtained from knowledge of concepts, while the 'habit' or 'associations' camp claims that all thinking and information can be clarified by either classical or operational conditioning from the single principle of creating stimulus-response ties.

Three other essential questions are raised by habit research.

- How many repetitions to implant a habit are necessary?
- Can a habit ever be completely lost once acquired?
- What's the best way of breaking a bad habit?

The first question does not have a single answer, but two significant developments have been made. Any repetition of an act appears to increase the strength of the habit somewhat, but the returns continue to decrease. This means we learn at the very beginning as fast as possible and should, therefore, be especially careful to start on the right foot. For example, in sports, it is advisable to get an expert's instruction so we can start forming the right habits at once. This prevents us from developing patterns that will have to be changed when it is incredibly difficult to do so.

Second, there is evidence that, without any repetition at all, certain behaviours can be formed based on single experiences. This appears to be the case where, as in traumatic experiences, emotions are involved. It may not extend to complex motor activities, although some parts may be established during the first trial, like the habit of placing one's foot on the clutch while driving a car. The topic of behaviour permanence has been explored for a long time.

Today, many psychologists believe that habits are never entirely lost, although more new or stronger habits can overlay them. There seems to be support for this hypothesis in the ease with which we revert to old motor behaviours like touch typing after many years — also in reviving old behaviour patterns in senile patients or individuals experiencing hypnotic regression (Ryder, 2014).

The problem can be answered, but not settled, at the moment of studying the memory process that potentially sheds some light on it.

Habit-breaking is another problem that cannot be solved with a single answer. The following are some of the most frequently discussed methods used by psychologists.

First, the incompatible-response:

Replacing the habit with a new antagonistic behaviour pattern. This approach is a way of 'counterconditioning' extinction— that is, by replacing it with a new one, it removes the initial response.

An example is a smoker who becomes accustomed to chewing when he feels like smoking. (Sometimes he ends up smoking and chewing at the same time!)

In applying this approach, as well as others, it is essential to follow the first two maxims suggested by William James in 1890: "We must be cautious about initiating an effort as deeply and determined as possible" and "Never suffer an exception until the new habit is firmly rooted in your life.

A boy caught smoking, for example, maybe forced to continue smoking until, essentially, he is ill. When this happens, the appetite for smoking will result in a new reaction, nausea, which will prevent the boy from continuing the habit.

For nail-biting, a similar technique can be applied. A form of fatigue is closely linked to 'deterrent treatments,' such as the use of Antabuse or hypnotic reinforcement in alcoholic addiction treatment.

Such approaches are types of behavioural therapy, like most habit-breaking strategies, and they do not seek to change the incentive that first created the pattern.

A method is toleration:

This is where a gradual introduction of stimuli raises an unwanted habit/reaction in small doses, so that more acceptable responses can be slowly established. For example, the child who fears grown dogs may react positively to a puppy, and this positive reaction will continue as he and the dog age; and eventually it will replace the fear. Likewise, through fun social experiences with one or two people, a shy person can sometimes overcome his timidity and gradually expand his acquaintances.

Kimble and Kendall (1953) found in animal studies that the method of toleration is superior to the method of exhaustion.

Another strategy is environmental change:

Getting away from the triggers or conditions that created a bad habit. This isn't always feasible — for starters, it's hard to get entirely away from smoking, and most people, just because they smoke, won't give up their old mates. Generally, a change of scene generates only temporary effects, although it may often work if the individual finds new satisfactions to replace those given by the original habit. This is counterconditioning again.

A good example is the approach of Alcoholics Anonymous. An essential part of the process is to find new leisure activities and new friends to make it unnecessary to seek other alcoholics' company or the bottle's companionship. Retribution is often used as a tool for breaking a habit, but it is probably the least successful of all methods. At best, it only briefly suppresses the undesirable habit, and usually only in the presence of the punisher. It does not encourage more favourable actions in itself and, instead, appears to be purely negative. However, it may perpetuate the bad habit; as a form of retaliation, the punished person may cling to it.

1.2 Difference between Habits and Addictions

In spite of unnecessary costs, addiction may be described as frequent involvement with anything due to a craving. This sounds like a habit, which also includes something done frequently. What are the dependency and behavioural variations and similarities?

Let's continue with some definitions of what looks like an addiction. After his first binge, a college freshman ends up in the emergency room but is not involved with alcohol again (although he may soon be). A pain control medical patient on opiates doesn't want the 'high' of the next injection but just seeks pain relief.

A low-stakes poker player has minor losses, but the gambling pleasure outweighs the cost to this individual. This last example shows that dependency depends heavily on the context in which it exists. It might not be as small a cost for one person as for another.

Now let's take the concept of addiction as an illness. The definition's 'three C's' are desire, effects, and (loss of) power. While commonly used, this definition's desire and control elements are inaccurate. The definition of the disease is all or none. You may or may not be an addict/alcoholic. There are several types of dependence, and in on all of them, you could be high, medium, or low. Where dependence starts is no clear dividing line. Second, it is understood that desire is uncontrollable. However, craving is entirely controllable with training. Otherwise, dependency is a state of hopelessness –but not!

Thankfully, everybody knows about the addictive behaviour's destructive consequences. The reason is that it's bad for you to switch an addictive behaviour! If you enjoy getting high, this increases the chances of harm to the body and mind, and eventually other areas of your life will also be negatively impacted.

We have a healthy addiction if the conduct in question produces more good than harm. A positive addiction is frequent involvement with a drug or behaviour, followed by a small amount of depression, with the benefits of participation outweighing the costs. The involvement of practice is compounded as costs and benefits are about the same. Interestingly, (harmful) addiction treatment requires successful addiction growth.

Seven hacks to change your habits in thirty days

Your life is controlled by what you focus on

- Tony Robbins

Chapter 2

This chapter provides a list of seven hacks by which you can easily change your bad habits and become the best you.

2.1 Realize the need to change

The first hack is to realize the need to change your bad habit. You understand that something is not right. This realisation happens when you get inspired by someone more successful or healthier than you. You want to be happy, healthy, and prosperous, like others. There are a few more factors that show signs that it's time to change your habits to fulfil your dreams.

2.2 Identify which habit to change

Now that you know that you need to change yourself to become a better person, the next step is to identify those habits that are harmful to you. The habit that creates difficulties for you in in the way of achieving your goals.

2.3 Replace the bad habit with a good habit

The third hack is to replace the identified habit with another that gives you same level of satisfaction; for example, if a person is trying to stop smoking, then he can chew gum if it gives him some pleasure. Then the bad habit can be replaced by gum; but if not, then you can try another habit and keep on trying different things until one gives you the same satisfaction.

2.4 Keep your willpower and motivation high

The purpose or why behind what you do is your motivation – in this case, it is behind the new habit you want. Motivation has different levels or layers with different strengths in each level or layer. Think of it as condensed circles. The circles like an onion in circles.

The outer layer is your big 'why' or motivating purpose.

Say you need to build some health and fitness habits: the big motivation of the outer layer is to be healthier and fitter as it makes you feel better, gives you more energy, gets you the most out of life, allows you to look better, all of which make you a happier person with stronger relationships.

Willpower is the power to put the will into action: to control what you are doing and to restrain yourself.

But the thing about will power is that you only have so much of it, and it's hard to rely on it when it runs out – because you are tired, hungry, or sad.

That's why you can wake up with a lot of willpower and good intentions, but it's harder to practice your will by evening.

2.5 Set goals

Setting goals is the process of choosing a target or objective you want to accomplish. Set smart goals that

- can be measured
- are attainable
- are appropriate
- are time-bound

2.6 Implementing plan measure your progress

Measurement is another secret to achieving long-term success of your goals. The human mind is fond of receiving feedback. Proof of our success is one of the most inspiring things we can encounter. That's why measurement is so critical to setting goals effectively. You gain insight into whether or not you are making progress by evaluating your performance.

A sample table of four weeks to change/track your habits

Days	Realization of	Identify bad habit	Replace habit	Motivation	Goal	Implementation	Meditation
M	If you are not	Eating too much	Shift to good	Write it down	Weight loss	Eat vegetable	Foe at least 5
T		Stay away	Try to eat grilled	Watch it in the	Measure your	Eat protein	Morning time is
W		Avoid going to	Eat baked			Eat more fruits	Go for a walk
T			Try oats instead of			Eat brown	If missed in the
F		Eat in portions	Try brown				
S			Take fresh				
S			Add lemon		Measure again	Veggie soup	
Mark green if			Make green tea				
Mark red if not							

Hack 1- Realize the need to change

Everyone thinks of changing the world, but no one thinks of changing himself - Leo Tolstoy

Chapter 3

Several factors force you to change yourself. When you are inspired by someone you try, or you wish you could be like, that person.

3.1 Inspiration

Anders Ericsson (1993) has been reminding us of the value of hard work for decades. The psychologist from the Florida State carried out a study that contributed to the so-called law of 10,000 hours. He and co-author Robert downplay the significance of native-born talent (even in people like Mozart) in their insightful new book, "Peak," in which is highlighted the importance of diligent practise - exhausting drills to refine your ability.

Anyone who has experienced excellence recognizes that Ericsson is fundamentally correct. The prerequisite for performance is hard effort. Yet there are times - after a lot of steady work and mastering the technical skills - when mind and spirit float. We call them inspiring moments.

Inspiration for what is a radical, countercultural, and spiritual movement is a much-used domesticated, amorphous, and secular term. Okay, bursts of inspiration according to normal logic don't make sense. They feel transcendent, irresistible, and uncontrollable. Time disappears or shifts its speed when one is motivated. The senses are strengthened. There may be goose bumps or shivering down the spine or feeling overwhelmed by beauty. Inspiration is always more important than pure admiration. There is an exciting feeling of acceleration, an energy blast, an understanding of expanded possibilities. The individual in the grip of inspiration has gained new insight and some holistic understanding, as if by chance, along with the feeling of being able to do more than what is expected.

Vladimir Nabokov believed in stages of inspiration. He wrote that there's the 'perfecting glow' and a 'tickly well-being' feeling that banishes all physical discomfort. The feeling is not yet giving up its identity, but a window has been opened, and some wind enters.

Then, after a few days, Nabokov continued that the writer 'feels what he's going to say.' There is a quick vision: the lightning bolt of inspiration that turns into a quick speech and a 'tumble of merging words' that forms the nucleus of a work that's going to grow from it over the months or years that follow.

An inspired job is different from normal life. First, as is usually understood, it's not about self-interest. A desire for money or promotion or prestige does not motivate it. The inspired person is driven by the work intrinsically. Such a person takes over the work.

Inspiration is not worth it. The time and effort invested prepare you for inspiration, but inspiration is a gift that goes beyond anything you might have deserved.

You can't control inspiration. Inspired people have lost some agency. They often feel that through them, something works, that some power is greater than themselves. The Greeks said there were the Muses. Believers may say it's either God or the Holy Spirit. Others might say it is a mysterious thing that bursts deep into the unconscious, as a new way of seeing.

Autonomous individuals don't get inspiration. It's a lovely contagion that goes through people. The word itself comes from the Latin, meaning "to breathe in." One inspiring achievement like the space program tends to elevate in others a sense of possibility; say, a little boy who dreams of being an astronomer. Then the inspired person performs his feats and inspires others, and so on. Inspiration is not solid and lasting. It's strong but short-lived; that's why so many people compare it to a wind. So people are waiting for his return when it's gone.

A Christian poet once wrote that inspiration is intrusive, transcendent, changing, yet also momentary and irregular. A poem can at once leave its author completely seized by nature and, in a deep way, separated from it; for as the act of making ends, the universe that seemed to overpower its limits becomes, once again, merely the world. It can be very difficult to retain confidence in that original moment of inspiration. That memory of that momentary blaze, and the art that emerged from it, can become a type of reproach to the fireless life in which you see yourself most of the time.

Most importantly, inspiration requires a certain posture, the kind that people feel when overwhelmed by something big and mysterious. They are both modest and self-assured, surrendering, and strong. We are willing to take a bold lark to something cool when inspired. We are bold enough to accept and try to express the craggy severity of reality in a new way.

Yes, to achieve this, hard work is really important. However, life is more mysterious than that.

3.2 Happenings that shows you need to change a habit

Life can be strangely complicated. You think you know what you desire; you've mapped it all out and your life probably isn't bad. However, you've settled, and your happiness fell by the wayside. These are key symptoms that you need a big life change. Whether you have been feeling like this for a few years or days, no one will lives their life just to go through the day. And let's be practical: You have more pressures and responsibilities, and you have to make major decisions. But it's tough. Running away and avoiding your life will not solve anything. Everything is usually determined by how you see the world and pick yourself up from a failure.

There is the notion that nothing is wrong with us, and we are filled with potential. We react to life situations, be they filled with trauma, stress, or dysfunctional relationships. Those who have faced/suffer at the hands of these life events the longest will not only grow more habitual to them, and build lower and lower expectations and dreams, but will also have less resiliency to handle change and stress. You have more energy and power than you give yourself credit for. However, if you're not exactly sure if your indifference has originated from your prevailing life condition or something else, there are symptoms that you need a significant life shift ASAP.

1. Your energy is low

When your strength is low from health issues, it's always best to visit the doctor. It could be as you're living a meaningless life, and you've just stopped caring. Maybe you have settled, and the idea of changing anything seems exhausting. You quit caring about yourself the way you once did. You require long walks, eating one healthy meal a day at least – trading off one junky snack for a healthy snack – and drink more water.

2. You feel paralyzed

Nothing inspires you anymore, and you don't recognize the last time you seriously laughed out loud. These little signs show you that you're not using your brains, so you can have a magnificent and interesting life. According to Mind Body Green, you might feel senseless because you have lost your passion and motivation. Try to do things that you like more often; it could help revitalize your soul.

3. You have stopped working on yourself

You are the most essential thing in your life, and it's crucial to remember to take care of yourself first because you won't be able to have a fulfilling life if you're not happy within. Go outside, research, start adopting 'me time,' and explore your world, be it through hobbies/activities with others. Try to find out and learn how vast your untapped abilities are. I can assure you that it will impress you.

4. Your environment is poisonous

If you find that you're with toxic people who always criticize you and your work, You are in a negative environment; it might be time to make some changes. It's difficult to be positive when your surroundings are not giving you happiness.

Your friends do not pump you up; rather, they enjoy listening to your down moments and require you to hear theirs regularly. In fact, they may celebrate your distress. They try to put you down in small ways that just don't feel right, but you may not be able to pinpoint situation - maybe it is the back-handed praise or someone cutting in when you are talking; maybe it is never showing up on time, not having remorse after a tiff, or treating you as a side person. In any case, such people waste your energy, resources, and tolerance.

5. You're not happy in your romantic relationship

Sometimes it's hard to admit that the one you are with isn't your romantic partner. Whether they are poisonous and bring you down, or your life goes on separate paths, it may be a good idea to stop fighting and just pull the plug. Your partner makes you feel less than you are in some way. They blame and use you as their emotional punching bag; and if it's physical abuse, then you need leave right now.

6. You're merely surviving

Losing yourself will ruin your imagination and motivation by doing the same mundane things. Going home from work and just paying the bills can be detrimental to the spirit. Your life should be packed with opportunities and challenges. Daydreaming about something you want without action is not going to get you far in life. If you felt anxious and excited, your gut might be telling you that you need a quick adjustment.

7. You have adopted a compulsive behaviour

You can't stop eating, smoking, or drinking. Compulsive behaviour is a sign that we're struggling to balance the voice of reason with the desires of your hearts. Addiction becomes a friend with whom you both celebrate and condone. Hold your vices apart and figure out the problem's origin so that you can fix it and live the life you have always wanted to live.

8. You're always dreaming of the past

Although remembering stuff is always good, you don't want to focus solely on the past because you're sick of your present-day life. According to the Huffington Post, Annabel Irion, a one hundred-year-old psychology and marketing professor at the University of Texas, an Art Marksman and Ph.D., if you look back on past events, you know how they worked out. Uncertainty is overwhelming. The present sometimes feels less fun than the past, because we're still waiting to find out how the different educational and business projects are going.

You keep on thinking that there has to be more than this. It may be time to change things around if you don't feel like its meaningful to your life. You may be looking for it or waiting patiently for signs for what it could be; but ultimately, if you are constantly waiting for the answers to come to you, you may never live your fullest life. Many people tend to wait for permission to live the life they've always dreamed of, according to the spiritual site Tiny Buddha, but no one else will give them access besides them.

9. While your life won't be filled with sunshine and butterflies

Every time you wake up, it shouldn't make you feel sad. Depression is your body and brain's way of saying that something has to change. It's there as a signal to make you stop and think again and hopefully do something else. You can start taking better care of yourself, saying 'no' to things or individuals that aren't healthy for you, seeking others' help, or changing your life situation. Whatever it is, it's one way to know it's time to change.

10. If your physical/mental health is deteriorating badly

It's time for a big change in your life. If there's one thing that's a sure sign of a need for improvement, it's stress. If you're living under immense stress at work, home, or in your social life, it's time to make a change. Change your habits like sleeping, dieting, and exercise. Be aware of how you interact with your body. Feeling worn out and drained is a crucial indication that, in some way, your life needs to be changed.

You will need to decide how you want to live your life, since no one else will. Pick yourself up, find out what you want, and go after it instead of feeling helpless and defeated. Don't forget to respect yourself, and don't settle. You deserve more than that.

3.3 Changing everyday habits will have an impact

Adapting to change: why it matters in our lives

The rule of life is change. Those that look only to the past or the present will surely miss the future, said John F Kennedy. We can't avoid it, and the tougher life gets, the more we resist change. Improvement according to Kennedy is a life policy. Transition surrounds us. It is the one thing that affects our lives the most drastically. As it will find you, there is no escaping transition. It will push you and pressure you to rethink how to live your life.

We're going to look at the significance of change and how you can adapt to an ever-changing life. Why do you have to change?

By chance, life doesn't get better; it gets better through change, says Jim Rohn. Change can come into our lives as a result of a crisis, a choice or just by chance. We're all faced with having to choose: will we make the change or not?

It's better to be ready for change as we have more influence over how we react to the changes we face in our lives. You have little control or options as to how you want to live your life when you are poorly prepared and slow to change. You are living your life as a conservative rather than a change activator.

Life is a series of spontaneous and natural changes. Do not fight them; it just causes sorrow. Let's make our reality. Let things flow naturally in whatever way we like says Lao Tzu. We can't avoid the unforeseen events (crises) in our lives, which are the events that challenge and force us to leave our comfort zone. When we neglect or hide from the challenge of change, the ability to learn and grow is denied to us.

To survive is to evolve; to change is to mature; to mature is to go on making oneself endlessly — Henri Bergson. Our resilience in life can only grow stronger if we accept change and handle difficulties in a positive way instead of hiding and neglecting the possibilities that change can bring.

The effect that change can bring into one's life is no escape. Managing life change is essential to living a life in which you not only survive but also succeed.

3.4 Adapting to Change Strategies

The five strategies below are key steps that will allow you to adapt and manage change successfully in your life.

1. Changing Your Mindset – Your Power Option

Change is impossible without improvement, and those who are unable to change their minds cannot change anything says George Bernard

Shaw. We are living our lives in our comfort zone. This is what our unconscious wants because it is the "known." Embracing change enters the unknown, and our subconscious doesn't like the "unknown," so it's going to resist it.

As we confront the destructive effects of transition, our anxiety and self-limiting values will kick into motion. The fact that change is a disruptor does not escape us, and it feels uncomfortable and frightening. However, it is a choice that allows us to bring about positive change.

We can't control the changing events in our lives, but we can control how we respond to the impact these events have on.

Life is a matter of choice. Some of us are sorry; some of us are proud. Some are going to haunt us forever. The message is: we are what we have decided to be (Graham). The more you use your decision power, and the more you concentrate your attitude on adapting to change positively, the more prepared you are to cope with the effect that change will bring to your life.

2. Find meaning in life: get out of your zone of comfort

Comfort zones are the enemies of achievement, where unrealized dreams are buried. 'Leadership starts when you step outside your comfort zone' - Roy T. Bennett. Knowing what's important gives you purpose and knowledge of how you want to live your life. You have insight and concentration with a sense of purpose and meaning, and these two elements are vital to be able to successfully adjust and handle the effect of change in life.

Having no purpose or meaning means that within the boundaries of your comfort zone, you continue to drift. The purpose and meaning of life give you the courage to leave your comfort zone, where you will experience change and the possibilities it can bring.

3. Let go of regrets

'The fact is, unless you let go, unless you forgive yourself, unless you forgive the circumstance, unless you know the situation is over, you can't move forward.' – Steve Maraboli. Regrets have a tremendous impact on how you respond to change, and they hold you back in life. It is significant to be able to move forward and let go of regrets.

It is the events of transition that create opportunities in life, so you may miss the possibilities of the present and the future if you look only to your past. You can't change what you have or haven't done, so let it go. The only power that you now have is choosing to live in a present and future life.

Blowing up a bunch of balloons and writing a regret on each is a great exercise to deal with disappointments in life. Then, let go of the balloons. As the balloons float away, say goodbye to regrets clearly.

This is a straightforward but effective way to deal with the pile of regrets you have gathered in your life.

4. Write a list of scary things to do–then go do them

Change is scary, and it's all about stepping into the unknown and out of your comfort zone. The unconscious wants to get out of our comfort zone and do frightening things. In reality, we want to train our subconscious to think that it is a normal thing to step out of our comfort zone and do scary things.

Make a list of scary things you'd like to do but were too afraid of. Put a plan in motion and do it afterwards. Go have fun, challenge yourself, and take advantage of the feeling of being frightened and entering the unknown.

Public speaking to me and many other individuals is one of the most terrifying things to do. The first speech was a nightmare to overcome my problem with public speaking. My knees were knocking (didn't know it was possible, but it is!), and when I started, I broke out in a sweat and my voice was a whisper.

I got through it, and although it wasn't the most celebrated speech, it was amazing to overcome my fear. I kept going and knew that I enjoyed talking so much to the public that I jumped at any chance to speak thereafter.

5. Maintaining the body in good health

'To keep the body in good health is a duty. Otherwise, you won't be able to keep your mind sharp and clear.' –Buddha

Living a balanced and active life builds resilience and the ability to successfully manage the disruption that change can have in your lives.

Stress is a normal response to everyday life changes and challenges. Stress can help you work better under pressure short term, but constant stress can present health problems. Finding positive ways to cope with the stress and pressure we face daily is key to physical and emotional survival.

Hack 2- Identify your bad habit

A habit cannot be tossed out of the window; it must be coaxed down the stairs a step at a time - Mark Twain

Chapter 4

Habits are the way the brain supports us by creating a pattern that neurons will obey. They put us on autopilot. They may be the slaves or masters of your life. Through promoting bad patterns, most people choose the latter. Instead of doing their job, they waste time before their smartphones or staring at TV screens.

Between presentations, they stress out because they cannot shake their procrastination.

We are struggling with weight and health because bad eating habits cannot be reversed. When we change, we feel good, but afterwards, we feel bad. We promise to break the bad habit, but are unable to resist temptation. We promise to do it until the idea disappears into tomorrow.

When you have bad habits, there's nothing to be sorry about: everybody's got bad habits. Being open to breaking them gives you an advantage over most people who deny them.

If you can't accept that something has to change, you can't change something.

Small, bad behaviours can have a negative long-term effect when piled up. In terms of productivity, your bad habits may create a dent.

Most are unable to acknowledge that the findings obtained today are the sum of what is repeatedly done. No wonder the power of habits only benefits a few.

4.1 The Power of Habits in our Lives

A young woman is walking into a lab. She has changed almost every part of her life over the past two years. She quit smoking, ran a marathon, and was promoted at work. Neurologists discovered that the patterns within her brain have fundamentally changed.

Procter & Gamble's marketers are studying videos of people who make their beds. They desperately try to sell a new product called Febreze, on its way to becoming the biggest flop in the history of the company. Immediately, one of the marketers notices an almost imperceptible pattern and Febreze manages to earn a billion dollars a year with a slight shift in ads.

An untested CEO takes over one of America's largest companies. His first business order attacks a single pattern among his employees - how they approach worker safety - and soon the company, Alcoa, becomes a Dow Jones top performer.

What's in common with all these people? By focusing on patterns that shape every area of our lives, they have achieved success. They succeeded in changing habits.

The award-winning business reporter for the New York Times, Charles Duhigg, takes us to the exciting edge of scientific discoveries that explain why there are habits and how they can be changed. Duhigg brings to life a full new understanding of human nature and its potential for transformation with penetrating intelligence and the ability to distil vast amounts of information into absorbing narratives.

Along the way, researchers learn why, despite years of trying, some people and companies are struggling to change, while others appear to be remaking themselves overnight. We visit laboratories where neuroscientists are investigating how habits work and exactly where they reside in our brains. We find out how the right habits have been crucial to the success of Michael Phelps, the Olympic swimmer, Howard Schultz, the Starbucks CEO, and Martin Luther King, Jr., the civil rights hero. They go inside

Procter & Gamble, Target Superstores, Saddleback Church of Rick Warren, NFL locker rooms, and the nation's largest hospitals and see how the adoption of so-called keystone behaviours can mean billions and the difference between failure and success, life and death.

The power of habit has a compelling case at its core: it's the secret to regular exercise, weight loss, raising excellent children, becoming more successful, creating innovative businesses and social movements, and achieving success. It's recognizing how habits work

Habits aren't fate. As Charles Duhigg shows, we can reshape our businesses, our communities, and our lives by harnessing this new science.

4.2 How Good Habits and Bad Habits are Formed

Habits are omnipresent, and we probably all think we know what a habit is. Wendy Wood is entirely right. More than 80% of people say they understand habits in conducted surveys. But when you change your actions, how effective are you? Can you make changes and stick to them? These same people say, 'Hmm, no, not very often.' Thus, they are not affected by what other people understand.

Habits are a tool for training. All we need to do is repeat something and get praised for it to develop a habit. In research, it has been found that in the same context, about 43% of what people do every day is repeated, usually while thinking about something else. They react automatically without making any real decisions. And that's the pattern. A habit is a kind of cognitive shortcut for doing what we have done in the past that has worked for us and given us some satisfaction.

Most of you think that self-control can force you to do things you don't want to do. Some people have super-will and others don't. Many people confuse their habits and self-control. In surveys, most say you have to exercise restraint to start a new habit, and that's just not true. The problem with self-control is that we all know people who are not effective in almost every area of their lives, and psychologists have built metrics to classify these individuals by assessing how much self-control they have.

The people on the survey scales that rank high tend to weigh less than the rest of us. They're more likely to have saved enough retirement money. They have happier relationships, and at work they're more productive, while at school, they get better grades. These things are connected to what we consider to be self-control. Yet recent research by Angela Duckworth and her colleagues has shown a curious contradiction: by exercising control, people who score high are not achieving success in life. By white knuckling through life, they don't practice self-denial. They know how to create patterns that meet their goals.

We consider that about 43% of what people do every day to be replicated, typically in the same way as if they're afraid of something. People who have high self-control instead are very good at developing the right behaviours to achieve excellent results in life. We seem to grasp the power of circumstances and choose those in which the desired behaviour are easiest to replicate. Such people don't have a lot of 'friction' in their lives, so they're not inclined to act counterproductively.

It feels that changing our self-control perspective can help us reclaim our sense of self-worth and become more childish. Instead of constantly berating ourselves – 'Oh man, I've done this thing again that I didn't want to do' - we should change our environment.

That's self-control's flip side. It's great to say, 'Yeah, I have a lot of self-control, and I'm excellent at resisting temptation,' but we fail so often and then feel like failures. It frees us from a very negative kind of life.

At M&M research teaches us how some of our health goals could potentially be undermined? It was a study of carrots and M&Ms (Pei-Ying Lin, 2015), In a computer game, people were asked to select carrots. When they were hungry and everyone played this game, and they got the carrots. Once they saw them on the screen, they had to push a joystick in the direction of the carrots, and then they won carrots and had to eat them. They all liked broccoli, but they also enjoyed cookies. And after they trained people to pick carrots by moving the joystick to the carrots whenever they saw them on the screen, they gave them the chance to pick M&M's if they wanted to. Now, people continued to select carrots when the screen was set up in the same way as during training. The carrots were chosen by more than 60%. But when the screen changed and the joystick had to be moved in a different direction, they stopped thinking and many went for M&M's.

It was found that people fall back on good as well as bad habits when they are distracted or feel unusually tired or overwhelmed.

This turns upside down the conventional thinking about habits. People think that patterns are bad things when they don't care about what they want. Yet they developed beneficial habits in the study to choose healthy food when they thought about it.

We generally think of top-down executive control as our 'good self.' But can pausing to think be the thing that prevents us from taking sustainable transportation or going to the gym if we had first set up those habits?

In many other studies, it was found that when people are affected or feel unusually tired or overwhelmed, they rely on good as well as bad habits. Their power over the executive is kind of off grid. They're worried about things going on in their lives or are too tired to make real decisions. We see both a boost in the performance of both good and bad habits. It is shocking because we like to believe that our self-conscious, executive regulation is well-intentioned and will help us achieve our goals.

Example of a woman

There are three sisters, and they all have young children. Their nieces and nephews were between two months and seven years of age. Young children can interfere with routine and lead to fewer repetitive behaviours for parents who, despite having young children, are trying to create good new habits.

One of the fascinating things that arose early in this study was that if one lives with other people, especially children, you have fewer overall behaviours than others simply because of the delays caused by the people in your life. An important thing was found when a mother with young children found a time and place to enjoy some control. It was 6:00 a.m. for her, as the children usually slept until 7:00 a.m. She used it for an hour of exercise and would go home in time to serve breakfast and send the kids off to class. At other times of the day, she tried to set up good exercise habits, and it just didn't work because the children always had to go to the doctor or to a friend's house or to practice or play sports. Unlike early in the morning, she didn't have much control over the rest of the day. So you must find the most consistent time of the day that is uninterruptedly yours and focus on building your habits there.

What tends to make it so difficult is the unforeseen situation of doing things automatically. We still make habits. For example, as part of their relationship, a husband and wife have many shared habits. They eat breakfast and dinner together. They have interconnected patterns, and these patterns are as important as the trends in the rest of our world. We debate the patterns we're trying to form with other people. And if we've been in a relationship that has ended, it's incredible how much our behaviour changes as that other person is no longer cueing the appropriate response. You miss the cue of your habit. It may not be a very romantic way of thinking about relationships, but it is a specific way of thinking.

Example of a girl

As a girl moved to a new city to start graduate school a year ago, she picked up a habit she always wanted: cycling as a primary form of transportation. Why is a transition or another big change in life, like the end of a relationship, a time to pick up good habits and break bad ones?

We find these changes in life to be very challenging, unwanted, and difficult; but they are opportunities as well. That thinking can get in the way, but it can also be an opportunity to begin to align our habits with our values.

Starting with restructuring your life takes some time, but when you no longer have those signals from your old background, you're freed up. Making new choices is like a window of opportunity.

Many of us may also have had the opposite experience of living in one place and developing a habit, but then we move and lose that routine and habit that had taken months or years to build. How resilient is changing habits, and is it essential to practice the new pattern for a long time? Well, time contributes to the strength of the habit, so the longer you've done something, the stronger the habits will be.

Research on transferring students to a new university has been done. What was found is that if the context at the new school is similar to the old one for those with strong habits, then they maintained their habits. People continue to exercise just as they did at their old university if they had a gym in both places; for example, in their apartment. They could just pick up the habit and go on. But if they moved to a new apartment without a gym, and there wasn't one nearby, or if there was only one running track and weights were usually lifted, they lost their habit.

One of the most important messages that all of us rely on is the context in which we live. Behaviours are usually based on what's comfortable and satisfying, i.e., what's easy for us to do over and over again and what's rewarding, It comes from our backgrounds and the places we live in. People across the country are witnessing different types of conditions in different states. We see people in the U.S. with different habits. People in Colorado, D.C., and Alaska, for example, exercise more than many other parts of the country, and they tend to be healthier as well. Some of this is that healthy people choose to go to those locations, but some of it is also that places affect us once we get there, prompting a better, more active lifestyle. And this has implications for our health and well-being.

All of us shape behaviours based on what's easy to do over and over again. The best proof we have is that forming a simple habit can take two to three months to make something so automated that you don't have to think about it.

A query is how often do I have to repeat something to make it a habit; and conventional wisdom is 21 days, but that's just not true. It's like when you begin to tie your shoes. You put on and tie your shoes, and you don't even have to will it. Instead, it seems to flow when you think of something else.

So, be patient and in it for the long haul, and don't give up.

Hack 3- Replace the bad habit

It is easier to prevent bad habits than break them - Benjamin Franklin

Chapter 5

The mind, like the body, embraces any habit you want to touch by practice --Socrates.

Habits are hard to alter because they are embedded within us. To make the action automatic, do things regularly to condition your neurons. That's why when you do your morning routine, your brain does not make a conscious effort. Bad habits are obstacles that divert you from your goals. They slow your progress.

A lot of people want to stop them. They are unable to improve despite their best efforts. They're taking their patterns to a place they don't want to.

Bad habits, as they make a person feel good, are hard to break. Dr. Russell Poldrack said that the patterns of pleasure are more challenging to break. When it experiences enjoyable behaviour, the brain releases the chemical dopamine. He said, if you do anything again and again and when you do it, the dopamine is there, and it makes the habit much deeper. Dopamine induces the urge to do it again when you don't do those things. 'People have different behaviours, so the way they break them is different from person to person'.

To nail what works for you, it takes a lot of trial-and-error. No one-size-fits-all formula can be followed by everyone.

Some science-based ways to help break or mitigate your bad habits:

5.1 Ways to Bid Your Bad Habits Goodbye

Identify your habit loop

While devouring a pack of chips or procrastinating, you have one bad habit you want to bid goodbye. When habits get formed, our brains work hard when we first participate in a new task- processing tons of new data as we find our way. But the behaviour begins to become automatic as soon as we understand how a task works, and the mental activity needed to do the job decreases dramatically.

Think about how much brainpower and focus you had to use when you first parked a car, or even when you tied your shoelaces for the first time. Equate that with the amount of mental effort you are making now.

Charles Duhigg (2014) writes, 'This process - in which the brain transforms a series of behaviours into an unconscious routine - is known as "chunking", and it's at the heart of how habits develop. There are thousands, if not hundreds, of behavioural chunks that we depend on every day.'

How Habit Loops Work

Habits consists of a simple, but compelling, three-step cycle. Per Duhigg, first, there's a cue, or a signal that tells the brain to go into automatic mode and use it. Then there is the routine that can be psychological or physical or mental. Finally, there's a bonus to help the brain find out if it's worth remembering this particular loop for the future. This chain becomes more and more automatic over time. The warning and reward are intertwined until a strong sense of anticipation and desire arises.

The first principle of habit-changing is that you have to play by the rules. That is, the three-step process (e.g., cue, routine, reward) doesn't escape since it is hard-wired into our minds. If you wish to get rid of a bad habit, you need to figure out how to execute a better routine and deliver the same reward. Let's presume that at the end of a long day you like to go out with your friends and have a few drinks. There are generally two benefits in this situation:

(1) The eventual socialization that happens and

(2) The alcohol's calming effects on your nervous system

These two incentives are both valid and appropriate. You'll still be miserable if you delete alcohol from your life but replace it with nothing else. The key is to keep the cue and the incentives (e.g., social time, relaxation) when adjusting the routine (e.g., drinking).

An alternative approach might be to convince a co-worker or friend after work to start exercising with you - running, yoga, rock climbing, or anything that works. You then have a balanced routine (exercise) replacing the unhealthy habit (drinking) while offering the same benefits.

If you wish to get rid of a bad habit, it is necessary to figure out how to implement a healthier routine to get the same reward.

How Habits Work

The hard thing about studying habit science is that most people want to know the secret formula to change a habit quickly when they hear about this field of research. When scientists discover how these patterns work, then it is fair that they also need to find a quick-change formula, right? If it were just that easy.

It's not that there are no equations; the challenge is that to change habits, there is not one equation. There are thousands.

Individuals and behaviours are all different, so the nuances of diagnosing and modifying patterns in our lives vary from individual to individual and behaviour to behaviour. Giving up smoking is different from curbing over-consumption, which is different from adjusting how you interact with your partner, which is different from how you perform work tasks. What's more, different cravings drive the habits of each person.

As a consequence, there is no one prescription offered in this book. Instead, I was hoping to offer something else: a structure for understanding how patterns work and a guide for playing with how they might change. Some behaviours make evaluating and influencing simple. Others are more complex and stubborn, requiring lengthy study. And for others, the transition is never a complete operation.

But that doesn't mean that it can't happen. It might not be quick to change, and it's not always easy. But with time and effort, it is possible to reshape almost any habit.

The framework:

- Identify the daily habit

- Take the incentive test

- Isolate the cue

- Have a strategy

Step one: identify the routine

Researchers found a simple neurological pathway at the heart of every habit, a loop consisting of three parts:

- a cue

- a routine and

- a reward

You have to identify the components of your loops to understand your habits. You can look for ways to replace old vices with new routines once you have diagnosed the habit loop of a particular behaviour.

As an example, say you have a problematic habit of going to the cafeteria and buying a chocolate chip cookie every afternoon. You've gained a few pounds from this habit - exactly 8 pounds - and your wife has made a couple of pointed remarks. You've also gone so far as to put a post-it on your screen that reads NO MORE COOKIES.

Yet you manage to ignore the note every afternoon, get up, walk to the cafeteria, buy a cookie, and eat it while sitting around the cash register with colleagues. It feels good, and it feels terrible afterwards. You promise yourself that tomorrow you will collect the courage to resist. It's going to be different tomorrow. But the habit retakes hold tomorrow.

How do you diagnose this behaviour and then change it? Through working out the pattern of the habit, and defining the routine is the first step. As with most behaviours, the most apparent thing in this cookie scenario is the attitude you want to alter. Your routine is to get up in the afternoon from your office, walk to the cafeteria, buy and eat a chocolate chip cookie while chatting with friends. So that's what you put in the loop. Next, a few less obvious questions are what's this routine's cue? Is that hungry? Are you bored? Low on energy? When you dive into another task, you need a break? And what is the payment? The cookie alone? The scene change? The threat of the temporary? Will you socialize with your colleagues? Or is it the power burst that comes from that sugar blast?

You should do a little research to work this out.

Step two: experiment with rewards

Rewards are efficient in their fulfilment of cravings. Yet, we are often unaware of the cravings that motivate our behaviours. When the marketing team from Febreze realized, for instance, that customers wanted a fresh smell at the end of a cleaning routine, they found a desire that nobody knew existed. In plain sight, it was hidden. Most cravings are like this: retrospectively obvious, but incredibly challenging to see when we're under their sway.

It is useful to experiment with different incentives and find out which cravings influence specific behaviours. It can take a couple of days, or a week or longer. You shouldn't feel any pressure during this time to make a real change; think of yourself in the data collection stage as a scientist.

If you feel the urge to go to the cafeteria to buy a cookie on the first day of your experiment, change your routine to provide a different incentive. For example, go for a walk outside, perhaps around the block, instead of going to the cafeteria and just return to your desk without eating anything. Go to the cafeteria the next day and buy a doughnut or a candy bar at your desk and eat it. Go to the cafeteria the next day, buy an apple and eat it as you talk with your family. Then, try a cup of coffee. Instead of going to the cafeteria, go for a few minutes to a friend's office to chat and go back to your desk.

You get the idea. What you choose to do is not as important as not buying a cookie. The aim is to test various theories to decide what causes the craving. Do you want the cookie itself, or do you want a break from work? If it's the cookie, are you hungry? (In which case an apple would work as well.) Or is it because you want the cookie's power burst? (So coffee should be enough.) Or, are you walking up the cafeteria as an excuse for socializing, and the cookie is just a convenient excuse? (If so, it should satisfy the temptation to walk to someone's office and talk for a few minutes.)

You may use an old trick to look for patterns when you test four or five different rewards: after each activity, jot down the first three things that come to mind when you get back to your desk on a piece of paper. These may be feelings, random thoughts, observations on how you feel, or just the first three words that come into your head. Then set the alarm for 15 minutes on your watch or phone. Tell yourself when time is up: do you still feel the urge for this cookie?

The explanation of why writing down three things is necessary is as follows. Even though they are meaningless words, they induces a momentary perception of what you think or feel. A note card loaded with comments can be a push into the consciousness of our desires, so writing three words will force a moment of focus. However, studies also show that writing down a few words helps us recall what we thought at the time. When we review our notes at the end of the experiment, remembering what we thought and felt at that precise moment will be much easier because our scribbled words will trigger a wave of memory.

And why the warning of 15 minutes? Because these tests aim to decide the desired reward. If you still have a desire to get up and go to the cafeteria fifteen minutes after eating a doughnut, then your addiction is not driven by a craving for sugar. If you still want a cookie after chattering at a colleague's desk, then the need for human contact is not what is driving your behaviour.

On the other hand, if you find it easy to get back to work fifteen minutes after talking with a friend, then you have recognized in the incentive a temporary relaxation and socialization that your addiction tried to fulfil.

You can isolate what you crave by experimenting with different rewards, which is essential in redesigning the habit. Once the routine and the reward have been worked out, what remains is to identify the cue.

Step three: isolate the cue

Approximately ten years ago, a psychologist at the University of Western Ontario tried to answer a problem that had puzzled social scientists for years: Why do some eyewitnesses misremember what they see, while others correctly recall events?

The eyewitnesses' memories are incredibly important, of course. And yet studies show that eyewitnesses sometimes misremember what they were doing. For example, when wearing a skirt, a woman may insist that the robber was a man or the crime occurred at dusk, while police reports say it happened at 2:00 in the afternoon. On the other hand, eyewitnesses will recall incidents witnessed with a near-perfect memory.

This phenomenon has been investigated by dozens of studies, trying to determine why some people are better eyewitnesses than others. Studies have theorized that some people simply have better memories, or that it is easier to remember a crime that happens in a familiar place. But those hypotheses were not checked; people with strong and weak memories, who are more and less familiar with a crime scene, are equally likely to misremember what happened.

A University of Western Ontario psychologist has taken a different approach. She wondered if researchers made a mistake by concentrating on what had been said by questioners and witnesses, rather than how they said it. She thought the interviewing process is affected by implicit signals. But she couldn't see anything as she watched videotape after videotape of witness interviews, looking for these signals. There was so much movement in each interview that she could not discern any trends: not the facial expressions, the ways the questions were asked, nor the fluctuating emotions.

So she came up with an idea: she drew up a list of a few things that she would concentrate o: the voices of the questioners, the witnesses' facial expressions, and how close the witnesses and questioners stood together. She then eliminated all details from those things that would confuse her. She turned up the volume on the television, so all she could sense was the sound of the questioners' voices instead of hearing words. She taped a paper over the faces of the questioners, so the expressions of the witnesses were all she could see. To measure their distance from each other, she put a tape measure on the monitor.

And once she began studying particular items, patterns kept jumping out. She saw that cops who used a soft, friendly tone were generally confronted by witnesses who misremembered evidence. Witnesses who smiled more or stood closer to the person asking the questions were more likely to misremember.

In other words, witnesses were more likely to misremember what had happened when environmental signs said 'we are friends'– as in a friendly voice or smiling face. Maybe it was because these signs of friendship subconsciously triggered a habit of pleasing the questioner.

The significance of this experiment is that dozens of other researchers had watched the same tapes. Many smart people had seen the same trends, but no one had understood them because each tape contained too much information to see a subtle cue.

But, once the psychologist decided to focus on only three behaviour categories and remove the alien data, the patterns leapt out. This is the same way we live our lives. The reason why it is so difficult to identify the indications that trigger our habits is that as our behaviours unfold while too much information is bombarding us. Tell yourself, do you eat breakfast every day because you're hungry at a particular time? Or because it says 7:30 on the clock? Or when did your kids start to eat? Maybe because you're dressed, that's when the habit of breakfast kicks in?

What causes the action when you turn your car left while driving to work? A sign on the street? A specific tree? In reality, it is the awareness that this is the right route. Are they all together? If you drive your kid to school, and you find that you've been absentmindedly on the path to work and not to school, what caused the mistake? What was the thought that made you 'drive to work', instead of the pattern of 'drive to school?'

We can use the same method as the therapist to locate a signal in the middle of the noise: defining groups of activities scrutinized to see trends. Luckily, in this respect, science provides some support. Experiments have shown that almost all the usual indications fit these categories:

- location
- time
- emotional state
- other people
- immediate preceding action

If you are trying to find out the cue for the habit of going to the cafeteria and buying a chocolate chip cookie, you should write down five things when the urge hits. These are my actual notes when I was trying to diagnose my habit.

- What time is it? (3:36 pm)
- What are you doing (sitting at my desk)?
- What is your state of emotion? (bored)
- Who else was there? (none)

- What was the previous action before the urge? (replied to an email)

The next day:

- Where are you? (returning the copier)

- What time is that? (3:18) and what is your state of emotion? (happy)

- Who else is there? (Jim from Sports)

- What was the previous action? (made a photocopy)

Day 3:

- Where are you? (meeting room)

- What time is that? (3:41 pm)

- What is your state of emotion? (I'm sick of the plan I'm working on)

- Who else is there? (editors come to the meeting)

- What was the previous operation before the urge? (I sat down because the meeting was about to begin)

It was pretty clear three days ago what cue activated my cookie addiction. I felt the need to get a snack at a particular time. I had already learned in step two that my conduct was not motivated by hunger. The bonus I was hoping for was a temporary distraction, the kind that comes from a friend's gossip. And the habit was activated between 3:00 and 4:00.

Step four: have a plan

Once you've worked out the habit cycle, you've established the incentive that activates your conduct, the stimulus that causes it, and the pattern itself so you can start to change your behaviour. By preparing for the cue and selecting an action that provides the reward you want, you will switch to a better routine. It's a plan that you need.

We learned in the prologue that a habit is a choice we make deliberately at some point and then stop thinking about it, but keep doing it, often every day.

To put it another way, a habit is a rule that our brain automatically follows: I will do a ROUTINE to get a REWARD when I see CUE (Charles Duhigg, 2014).

We need to start making decisions again to re-engineer the equation. And, according to study after study, the easiest way to do this is to have a strategy. Such preparations are known as 'implementation goals' within the field of psychology. Take, for example, my afternoon cookie addiction. By using this method, I discovered that in the afternoon, my cue was at about 3:30. I knew my routine was going to the cafeteria, buying a cookie, and chatting with friends. And, through experimenting, I discovered it wasn't the cookie I wanted: it was a moment of fun and a chance to socialize.

So, I wrote a plan: I'm going to go to a friend's office every day at 3:30 and chat for 10 minutes. I fixed the alarm on my watch for 2:30 to make sure I remembered. It wasn't working right away. I was busy for a few days, ignored the warning, and then fell off the wall. Sometimes, having a friend willing to talk seemed like too much hassle: it was easier to get a cookie, so I gave up on the desire. But on the day that I followed my plan - when my alarm went off - I forced myself to walk to a friend's office and talk for 10 minutes. I found that I was feeling better at the end of the working day. I didn't go to the kitchen and didn't eat a cookie, so I felt pretty good. Finally, it got automatic: I found a friend when the alarm rang and ended the day feeling a real sense of achievement. I didn't think about the routine after a couple of weeks. Then I went to the cafeteria, bought tea and drank it with friends when I couldn't find anyone to talk to.

That was all-around six months ago. I no longer have to look at my watch at some point. But I'm absentmindedly standing up at around 3:30 every day, searching the newsroom for someone to talk to, wasting 10 minutes chattering about the news, and then returning to my office. It's happening almost without knowing about it. It has become a custom.

5.2 It's not that "I can't," But "I Don't."

Houston University researchers conducted an experiment in which one group was instructed to use 'I can't,' while the other used 'I don't.' A granola bar or some chocolate was given after the test. 39% of people who used 'I can't' selected the granola bar, while it was preferred by 64% of people who used 'I don't' instead of chocolate.

This experiment shows the importance of choosing a word and how it can affect a person's motivation. Rather than thinking, 'I can't eat potato chips,' reframe it as 'I don't eat potato chips.' It's kind of telling yourself you're not doing the behaviour.

If they answer with 'I can't', most people are easily convinced by others.

Are you acquainted with it?

'Check this here. Only one glass of beer.' 'No, that's not something I should drink.' 'Oh, don't be a child. You will not be destroyed by one shot.' 'I can't. I can't do that. Yeah, just one.' Unlike: 'I'm not drinking beer. My body's not reacting well.'

5.3 Replacing the Bad Habit with a Good Habit

It can be hard to stop something. Psychologist Timothy Pitchy (Maltz., 1960) said a new pattern must be developed to break a bad habit. The neurons in the brain follow a pattern as behaviours are established that make the task easier to perform. It's hard to break this cycle. To weaken it, you need to create a new habit.

Gradually, the neurons will create a new relationship that becomes a habit when the activity is continuously fostered.

Neuroscientist Elliot Berkman also states that it is safer for the brain to do something different than avoid doing the same task without being replaced.

Start thinking about those changes now if you want any to happen. Expose yourself to materials and educate yourself on the subject. You are thus preparing your subconscious for the transition you are about to launch.

The longer you have the habit, the more difficult it will be to break it.

5.4 Activate the Red Traffic Light in Your Brain

There are two types of cells with approximately equal numbers, one that activates the 'go' signal. One of Duke University's researchers, Nicole Calakos, taught mice to grow behaviours. clicking a button, the mice were trained to get a treat.

They contrasted the educated mice's brains with those of untrained mice and found patterns. They found that there are other 'stop' signals. It is easier for untrained mice to avoid them when their 'stop' warning came first. The trained mice's brains initially triggered the 'go' signal due to the habits they developed.

The go mechanism is powerful when behaviours are repeated and triggered. Reducing activity exposure can slowly decrease the brain's 'go' signal capacity. It's good to break bad habits. The go signal is not reinforced as much when you remember to stop the actions. The habit is low when the go signal does not work regularly.

5.5 They Will Break You or You Break Them

"Cultivate only the behaviours you're able to master." — Elbert Hubbard It can be challenging to alter what you always do and most people don't need to do it. Those who are not easily discouraged will conquer them.

Habits can work for your benefit. They will make you work more quickly. In any task you choose to do, you can be successful.

Yet habits can also harm your growth. To reach their goals, many people are paralyzed; they're letting go of bad habits. We do not practice muscle control that is immune to temptations.

World champions are people willing to sacrifice the comfort they need to win. It can be difficult at the onset to break bad habits. But when you feel the pain and suffering of the workout, you become a winner. You will bounce back and heal the damage caused by bad habits.

If the first attempt doesn't work, that's perfect. Let your mistakes inspire you to redouble your efforts, create new habits, and search for opportunities to better yourself.

You are stronger and more capable of confronting the next step as you resolve your challenges.

Such bad habits are now part of history before you know it. They're no longer getting in your way. They are not enslaving you. They're not dictating your acts.

Instead, you are leading the way.

Hack 4- Keep your will power and motivation high

Strength does not come with physical capacity. It comes from an indomitable will - Mahatma Gandhi

Chapter 6

Concerning a situation or action, achieving our goals is more the product of our daily behaviours than any dramatic circumstance or effort on our part. Habits are a vital part of mind control because your subconscious uses habits as a shortcut or power-saving tool if you use the power of habits to manipulate your mind effectively. Rather than viewing habits as something we need to control and overcome in a negative light, they are an empowering tool to enhance our lives, helping us make changes, thereby making us happy.

To do this, we have to know which habits are good for us, and which habits do not help achieve our goals. Therefore, the first step is to recognize a habit that you want to change for a useful, inspiring, optimistic, good or excellent habit, a new habit you want to develop.

This is a significant step as we are not all conscious of them. We have to take a deliberate look back and recognize the habit or accept that what we tend to do but would like to alter is a repetitive way of reacting.

6.1 Willpower

Now that you know the habit you want to change, do you use your willpower to change it and your motivation to keep it going?

Yes and no. Yes, because both have an essential role to play when it comes to willpower habits and motivation, but they are not enough on their own: there are limitations to be aware of.

Willpower is the power to put will into action to control what you are doing and to restrain yourself. But the thing about will power is that you only have so much of it, and it's hard to rely on it when it runs out – when we are tired, hungry, or sad. That's why you can wake up with a lot of willpower and good intentions, but it's harder to practice your will by evening.

Although the more we do it, the more determination we have to get stronger; and the brain likes your patterns, so it wants to keep them.

So, while willpower has a role to play in improving behaviours, you can't rely on doing it alone. The same applies to inspiration. Think of some habits you've tried to change in the past but couldn't do it and ask yourself honestly why you couldn't? Did you give up on the first sign of trouble? We can never use an excuse in this day and age with so much online information available. Think about it: if you want to lose weight, start a blog, or open a business, all that is required is to Google it, and you'll find thousands of people telling you how to do it step by step. The real reason we don't have what we want is that we are always waiting until we 'feel like doing it,' but the harsh reality is that you will never feel like it. There's no motivation coming, and no one will make you do anything. You've got to do it yourself. Remember the rule of 40% and push yourself past your comfort zone.

You used to think that you will eventually feel like doing something if you want to. You used to think there was going to be inspiration from somewhere. But you'll find that you'll never feel like doing the hard things in life. Think of it: no one ever feels like going on a diet and no one ever feels like getting out of a comfortable warm bed an hour early. If you want to make your ambitions become reality, whether you like it or not, you have to do things. If you're going to make a change in your life, you'll have to do it at the beginning of a new habit you are developing or over any bad habit you want to break. It's going to be hard. It's sudden inspiration and it doesn't last. Emotions are fleeting; they also won't last. Your job is to do the stuff you don't want to do so you can have all you want in life.

We must stop lying to ourselves by saying, 'I'm going to start tomorrow,' because if you don't feel like doing something today, you're not going to feel like doing it tomorrow either.

The difference in those who succeed and unsuccessful people is that they do what's required to get to the goal. The ineffective do what relieves anxiety. Successful people do what they think they ought to do, and whether they like it or not, they act.

Think of muscle endurance. It's accurate until it's gone. When you first start using a muscle, it has a limited amount of endurance, but the more you use it over time, the better it becomes. As Charles Duhigg puts it, 'as people in one part of their lives strengthened their willpower muscles - in the gym or a money management program - that energy was poured into what they ate or how hard they worked. When willpower got stronger, it affected everything. 'That's why it's so effective to make tiny one percent changes. If you are left with VERY little willpower in the tank, you can STILL improve one percent because the perceived difficulty is so low. Therefore, once you go, you will continue to use the 40 percent rule.

You have only one life to live, and you deserve to achieve all you want in life, but if you're waiting to 'feel like it' before you change your bad habits, you'll be waiting forever. As Stephen Guise put it, 'Don't imagine the easiest days when it comes to personal change; imagine the toughest days. If you are tired, stressed, and very busy on the day you can do something; you can do it every day.'

6.2 Motivation

The purpose or 'why' is the motivation behind the new habit you want. Motivation has different levels or layers and different strengths in each. Think of it as condensed circles: circles as in an onion. The outer layer is your significant 'why' or the motivating purpose.

When establishing health and fitness habits, the big motivation of the outer layer is to be healthy and fit as it makes you feel better, gives you more energy, gets you the most out of life, makes you look better as a happier person. It also helps you form better relationships.

You need to develop healthy habits because it feels good to be fit and healthy, making you a happier individual. That's all very well and good, since it's challenging to keep it in the forefront of our minds, and we know that determination will only take us so far, especially when we step into the next layer.

Your condition is the next layer or circle in the onion. For example, you have a busy life, you look after your house, you have a family, a hectic social life, or a lot of commitments, and you're always rushing from one thing to the next.

You arrive at the next layer in which your career or job requires a lot of energy and time from you. Then comes the final layer because a circle represents you right in the middle (like the bullseye on a dartboard). It's written in it the word 'you' of 'me.' This is you when you are talking about this very moment or the present moment.

That's the pattern, but it's not static, because the thickness of these layers varies over days and week; they differ from a Monday morning to the weekend. The idea is your inspiration; it begins with the best of intentions as you pass through the layers.

The morning often starts with good intentions of improving habits; however, you get busy getting breakfast finished and going to work, so the motivation dips and then you in the middle circle – you not so concerned about the broader picture because the needs of the moment are closer to you than the big circle on the outer side. Maybe the needs of the situation are that you're hungry, you're busy and you need something fast to improve your strength; but more importantly to conquer the hunger and do it quickly and easily in a satisfactory way. That's when you don't just focus on willpower and inspiration to support you.

To see what this might be, we need to go back to the idea of what a pattern is. The surprising thing about motivation is that it often comes after starting a new action, not before. We have the common misconception that the consequence of passively watching a motivational video or reading an inspirational book is an inspiration. Active inspiration, however, can be a much stronger motivator.

Motivation is often the outcome of an action, not its cause. Getting started is a type of powerful motivation that naturally generates momentum, even in tiny ways.

Start easy

This phenomenon is referred to as Productivity Physics because it is essentially Newton's First Law applied to habit formation: objects in motion tend to remain in motion. Once a task has started, it is easier to continue moving it forward. Once you have begun a behaviour, you don't need much motivation. Almost all of a task's stress is at the outset. Progress happens more naturally after you start. In other words, completing a job is often simpler than beginning it. Therefore, one of the keys to motivation is to make an easy start.

6.3 How to Get Motivated and Take Action

Most people struggle to find the motivation they need to achieve the goals they want because certain aspects of the process are consuming too much time and energy. If you're going to find motivation easier and get started, it helps to automate your behaviours in their early stages.

Schedule your motivation says Sarah Peck. Many people never get around to writing because they're always wondering when they're going to write next. You can say the same thing about working out, starting a business, creating art, and building most habits.

If exercising doesn't have a time it usually happens, then every day you're going to wake up thinking, 'I hope I feel motivated to practice today'. If your company doesn't have a marketing strategy, then you're going to show up at work crossing your fingers that you're going to find a way to get the word out (in addition to everything else you need to do).

If you don't have a set time to write every week, you'll find yourself saying things like, 'I just want to find the energy to do it'. An article in The Guardian explained the situation: 'If you're wasting resources trying to decide when or where to work, you're going to hinder your ability to do the job.' This makes it simpler for you to follow through, regardless of your level of motivation. And there are plenty of determination and motivation research studies to support this statement.

Stop waiting for your motivation or inspiration to hit you and set a timeline for your behaviours. There is a contrast between amateurs and professionals: professionals set and stick to a timetable, while amateurs wait before they feel motivated or inspired.

6.4 How to be Motivated When You Don't Feel like It

How do some of the world's most prolific artists get motivated? They are not just setting plans; they are creating routines.

Twyla Tharp is widely considered one of the modern era's most celebrated dancers and choreographers. Tharp addresses the role habits or routines of a pre-game have played in her success: She continues a ritual every day of her life; she wakes up at 5:30 a.m., puts on her workout clothes (leg warmers, sweatshirts, and hat). She leaves her Manhattan home, hails a taxi, and tells the driver to take her to the 91st Street Pumping Iron Gym on First Avenue, where she works out for 3 hours. The ritual of stretching and weight training is not what brings her in the gym each morning; the cab is the ritual. The habit is finished the moment she tells the driver where to go.

It's a simple act but performed the same way every morning - making it dull and quick to do. It reduces the chance of skipping it or doing it differently. It's one more thing to worry about in the list of habits, and one less.

Many other well-known creatives have routines. Writer Mason Currey states that many of the world's great artists follow a consistent schedule in the book, Daily Rituals: How Artists Work.

Maya Angelou rented a local hotel room to write. She arrived at 6:30 a.m., wrote to 2:00 p.m., and then went home to edit. At the hotel, she never slept.

Michael Chabon, the recipient of the Pulitzer Prize, writes five nights a week between 10:00 p.m. and 3:00 a.m.

At 4:00 a.m., Haruki Murakami wakes up, writes for five hours, and then goes for a run.

Top creatives' work is not motivated or inspired but follows a consistent pattern and routine. Here are some examples of how ritual and method can be used to get motivated: exercise more consistently and use the same routine in the gym to warm up.

- Make yourself more creative: follow a creative ritual before starting to write or paint or sing.

- Start stress-free every day: create a ritual of meditation for five minutes in the morning.

- Get better sleep: follow the routine of 'powering down' before bed.

A ritual's power, or a pre-game routine, is that it's a mindless way to initiate a behaviour. It makes it easier to start habits, and that means it's easier to keep doing consistently.

The key to any good ritual is to remove the need for decision-making. What should I do first? When do I have to do this? How am I going to do this? Most people never move because they are unable to decide how to get started. You want the behaviour to be comfortable and automatic, so when it becomes difficult and challenging, you have the strength to finish it.

How to Make Motivation a Habit

There are three simple steps to build better routines and make motivation a habit.

Step 1:

Starting with an excellent pre-game routine is so simple that you can't say no to it. To begin your pre-game routine, you shouldn't need motivation. My writing routine, for example, begins with getting a glass of water. My weightlifting routine begins with putting on my lifting shoes. I can't say no to them; these tasks are so simple.

Starting is the most significant part of any task. In the beginning, if you can't get motivated, you will find that motivation always comes after you start. That's why you need to start your pre-game routine incredibly fast.

Step 2:

You can step toward the end goal with your routine. There is often a lack of mental motivation associated with limited or no physical movement. Picture your physical condition when you feel depressed, lonely, or unmotivated. You're not going. You may be slumping over like a glob, melting painfully into the sofa.

The opposite is true, as well. If you're physically moving and involved; you're much more likely to feel mentally engaged and healthy. For starters, when you're dancing, it's almost impossible not to feel lively, awake and energized.

While it should be as easy to start your routine, it should gradually change into more and more physical movement. Your physical movement will follow your mind and motivation. It's worth noting that exercise doesn't have to mean physical movement. For instance, if you aim to write, you should be brought closer to the physical act of writing in your routine.

Step 3:

Every time you have to follow the same pattern. Your pre-game routine's primary purpose is to create a series of events that you always execute before you perform a particular task. The pre-game routine tells the mind, 'This is what's going on before I do.' The routine is embedded in your success such that you're drawn into a mental state that's ready to succeed by merely performing the routine. You don't have to know how to find inspiration; just continue your routine.

You may know that your pre-game routine is essentially making a 'reminder' for yourself. Your pre-game routine is the catalyst that sets off a habit, even though you are not inspired to do it.

This is vital because it's often too much effort to find out what you should do next when you are not motivated. You will often decide just to quit when faced with another decision. However, the solution is the pre-game routine, so you know exactly what to do next. There is no discussion or decision-making. There is no lack of motivation. You're just following the pattern.

How to Stay Motivated for the Long-Run

We've covered a few strategies to make getting motivated and starting a task easier. What about keeping the long-running motivation? How can you be motivated to stay well?

How to Stay Motivated with the Goldilocks Rule

Say you're a tennis player. You'll quickly get bored if you play a serious match against a four-year-old. It's too easy. If you try to play a serious game against a professional tennis player like Roger Federer or Serena Williams on the opposite end of the spectrum, you're likely to become demotivated for another reason: it's too hard.

Compare these encounters to playing tennis with someone you're equal to. You win a couple of points as the game progresses and you lose a couple of points. You've got a chance to win the match, but only if you're trying. Your concentration is narrowing, distractions are fading away, and you are fully committed to the task at hand. The obstacle you face is 'only manageable.' There's no guarantee of success, but it's possible. Science has found that activities like this are the most likely to keep us motivated in the long run.

People like challenges, but only if they are within the optimum difficulty range. There are tedious tasks significantly below your current skills. Tasks that surpass your current capabilities substantially are frustrating. Yet job is right on the edge of success and failure empowers our human brains tremendously. We just want to develop talent beyond the present horizon.

We may call this the Goldilocks phenomenon. The Goldilocks Rule states that when taking on projects on the edge of their current abilities, people experience optimum motivation (Stillam, 2016). Not too complicated. It's not that easy. It's about correct.

One of the keys to retaining long-term motivation is focusing on projects that conform to the Goldilocks rule. If you feel unmotivated to work on a task, it is often because it has drifted into a boredom area or far exceeds your ability. You need to search for a way to pull your tasks back to the limit where you feel challenged but capable.

How to Reach Peak Motivation

Sometimes the beautiful combination of joy and peak output is called flow. Flow is what athletes and performers feel when they're 'in the zone.' Flow is the state of mind you experience when you're so focused on the task that the rest of the world vanishes away.

We might define flow as your highest motivation state in many ways. You'd be stressed to find a time when you're more motivated to take on the job you're working on.

One concern of researchers is whether or not you obey the Goldilocks Rule mentioned earlier. If you are focusing on optimally difficulty tasks, not only will you be inspired, but you will experience a boost in happiness. As psychologist Gilbert puts it, 'One of the major sources of human happiness is working on tasks at an acceptable level of difficulty, neither too hard nor too easy." Moreover, to achieve this peak performance, you need not only to work on challenges at the correct level of difficulty but also assess your immediate progress. One of the keys to entering a flow state, as psychologist Jonathan Haidt states it, is that 'you get instant feedback on how you are doing at each stage.' So we can conclude that evaluation is a crucial factor in motivation. Put it more simply, two of the most critical components of peak motivation are meeting an optimum challenge and getting immediate feedback on the progress you are making towards this goal.

What to do when inspiration eventually drops at some stage: the desire to do a job will slip. If inspiration disappears, what happens? Don't expect to have all the answers, but when you feel like giving up, here's what to remember.

Your Mind is a Suggestion Engine

Consider as a suggestion, not an order, every thought you have. For example, as I'm writing this now, my subconscious says that I'm tired. It suggests that I give up. This may mean that I'll take a more natural path.

But, if I am still in the moment, I will find new ideas. My mind always says that once it's done, I'll feel very good about doing the job. This means that when I stick to the plan, I respect the image I am creating. This means I can complete the mission, even if I don't feel like it. None of these are instructions. They're just options. I can choose which option to follow.

Discomfort is Temporary

Compared to the time you spend on your regular day or week, almost any activity you do is done quickly. You'll finish your workout in an hour or two. Tomorrow morning, your message will be typed for completion.

Life is now better than ever before. If you weren't harvesting your food and building your own house 300 years ago, you'd die. Today we whine about our iPhone charger being forgotten.

Keep your perspective. Your life is a great and temporary inconvenience. Step into this uncomfortable moment and let it reinforce you.

Once it's done, it's done. Theodore Roosevelt famously once said, 'Far away, the best prize life has to offer is the opportunity to work hard at work worth doing.' So often it seems we want to work efficiently. We want to be supported and valued in our work, but through it, we don't want to fight. We desire our stomachs to be flat and our arms to be muscular, but if this means doing another workout, we don't want the grind. We want the outcome, but not the preceding failed attempts. In short, we want the gold, but not the grind.

Most want gold medals. Few train like an Olympian. And yet, despite our resistance to it, after the hard work was done, you never felt worse. There are days when starting is damn hard but finishing is always worth it. Sometimes, a victory worth celebrating is the easy act of just showing up. That's half the battle, and then having the courage to do the work accomplishes the full goal when you go all the way.

This is Life

Life is a constant balance between succeeding distractions and overcoming the stress of discipline. It is not an exaggeration to say that in this delicate balance, our lives and personalities are established. What is life if not a multitude of numerous daily battles, small decisions and momentary victories?

The moment when you don't want to do the job is not a moment to throw away. This moment is just as much your life as any other moment. Spend it so you're going to be proud.

Hack 5- Set your Goals

If you want to be happy, set a goal that commands your thoughts, liberates your energy and inspire your hopes.
-Andrew Carnegie

Chapter 7

7.1 What is goal setting?

Many goal-setting exercises begin with an overpaid consultant standing next to a whiteboard and asking something like, What do you see as success? What do you want to do in precise terms? However, if we are serious about our goals, we should start with a very different question. Instead of considering what kind of success we want, we should ask: What kind of pain do I want? This is a strategy I learned from Mark Manson, the author. What Mark found is that it is natural to have a target. Who wouldn't want to write a bestselling book, lose weight, or earn more money? Everyone wants to accomplish these goals.

The real challenge is not to decide if you want the outcome, but to make the compromises necessary to achieve the goal. Would you like the lifestyle of your quest? Would you like the dull and ugly cycle that comes before the glamorous and exciting result?

Sitting around and talking about what we can do or what we would like to do is easy. Accepting the trade-offs that come with our ambitions is an entirely different matter.

It takes us to our first insight into the answer. Goal setting is not just about picking the benefits you want to reap, but also about the cost you're willing to pay.

Rudders and Oars

Imagine a little boat. Your target is like the boat's rudder. They set the course and decide where you're going. If you commit to one goal, the rudder will remain in place, and you will continue to move forward. If you flip-flop between targets, the rudder moves all around, and rowing in circles.

Another part of the boat, however, is even more critical than the rudder: the oars. If your goal is the rudder, the poles will be your way to achieve it. Although the rudder decides your course, your speed is determined by the oars.

The rudder and oars metaphor helps to clarify the distinction between structures and priorities. It is an important distinction that exists everywhere in life.

• Your goal is to win the championship if you're a coach. Every day, the program is what the team is doing in practice.

- If you're an author, you're meant to write a novel. Your routine is the system of writing every week.

- You're running a marathon if you're a runner. Your program will be your monthly training schedule.

- If you're an entrepreneur, creating a million-dollar business is your dream. Your application is your method of sales and marketing.

Objectives are useful in setting the course. Systems are great for making real progress. The most significant advantage of having a target is that it shows you what kind of structure you need to set up. The system itself, however, consists of what the results have been achieved.

This takes us to our second insight into the answer. Goals determine the direction in which you are heading. Programs determine your success. Gripping the rudder, you'll never get anywhere. You've got to row.

7.2 How to Set Goals You'll Follow

Okay, now that we've addressed the trade-offs and structures that come with goals. Now let's think about how you're going to set goals.

There are three basic strategies in setting goals:

1. Ruthlessly eliminate your goals

Psychologists have a term they call 'target rivalry.' Target competition means that the other goals you have are the biggest obstacles to achieving your goals. In other words, for your time and attention, your targets compete with each other. You have to pull focus and energy from your other pursuits whenever you pursue a new goal. This is essentially the theory of the Four Burners in action. You have to turn down the others when you turn one burner up.

There's good news now. One of the great ways to make progress toward your goals is to stop and concentrate on less important things. Sometimes you just need to reorganize your goals a little bit, and instant change comes much quicker as you are now fully committed to a target that had previously received only moderate attention.

This is a valuable insight. Typically, when we don't achieve our goals, we think our goal or approach was wrong. Experts say, You've got to think bigger! Choose a vision that's so huge that it's going to motivate you every day. Or we're thinking, If only I've had more hours in the day! These excuses cloud the more significant issue.

What often looks like a goal-setting problem is actually a goal selection issue. It is not bigger goals that we need, but a better focus. You have to choose one thing and do away with everything else ruthlessly. In Seth Godin's words, 'You don't have to take more time, and you just have to know.'

Our lives are like rose bushes. They establish more buds than they can sustain as they grows. If you're talking to an experienced gardener, they'll tell you that you need to prune rose bushes to bring out the best in both their appearance and production. In other words, if you want a rose bush to thrive, then some of the good buds need to be cut off so that the great ones can blossom ultimately.

The priorities are identical. The bushes need to be cut and trimmed consistently. It's natural for new goals to join our lives as we get excited about new opportunities — just like adding new buds is natural for a rose bush. If we can have the confidence to prune a few of our goals, then we will create the space needed to thrive for the remaining goals. Inclusive growth and optimal living need pruning. If you've decided to alter a habit - whether you're quitting smoking, reducing your blood pressure, becoming more involved, or doing something else to improve your health-it is the first step towards making a change.

1. Have your justification

It's imperative to know why you want to change a habit. You may want to stop smoking so that future health problems can be avoided. Perhaps you'd like to eat a healthy diet to lose weight. The purpose may be evident if you have high blood pressure.

To make a change, you need to feel ready. If you're not feeling ready now, that's all right. You can still think and plan. You're prepared for the next step if you want to make a change.

Changing habits is not easy. Yet taking the time to think about what is going to motivate or inspire you will help you achieve your goals.

2. Set goals that you can reach: SMART goals

You've probably already learned about SMART goals. But do you apply the rule at all times? The simple fact is that goals should be built strong to be SMART. Whatever SMART stands for (there are many variants) but the core is that targets should be general.

- Measurable

- Attainable

- Appropriate

- Time-bound

Set Clear Objectives

The goal must be straightforward and well established. Vague or generalised targets are unhelpful, as they do not provide enough guidance. Remember that they show the way; you need goals. Make it as simple as you can by deciding where you want to end up. .

Set Measurable Goals

Include correct numbers, times, and so on for your goals so you can calculate your progress. If your target is described simply as 'Reducing expenses,' how do you know when you've been successful? If you have a one percent reduction in a month, or a ten percent reduction in two years? You will lack the joy that comes with knowing you've achieved something without a way to measure your performance.

Set Realistic Goals

Make sure the goals you set can be accomplished. When you set a goal, you have no hope of achieving; you're just going to demoralize yourself and erode your confidence.

When you are certain about your reasons for wanting to make a change, it's time to set your goals.

- **Long-term targets**: These are the big goals you would like to accomplish in 6 to 12 months.

- **Short-term targets:** What are the short-term priorities that will help you achieve your long-term aims? Short-term objectives are the small steps to improve your health week after week.

- **Revised goals:** Chart your progress and change your goals as you move forward to help you stay motivated.

To set goals, use these tips:

- **Focus on small goals**: This will motivate you overtime to reach larger goals. You're going to have more success with smaller goals, which will help you stay with it.

- **Write down your priorities**: The actual act of writing down a goal makes it concrete and real. You don't have any excuse to forget that. Use the word 'will' instead of 'would' or 'might' as you write. For example, 'I'm going to cut my operating expenses by ten percent this year, not 'I'd like to cut my operating expenses by ten percent this year.' The first target statement has power, and you can 'see' yourself cutting expenses; the second lacks passion and gives you an excuse if you're side-tracked.

This will help you remember and give you a clearer picture of what you want to do. Use a personal action plan to chart your goals. Hang up your project-plan, and you'll often see it as a reminder of what you're trying to do.

- **Specify your targets**: You will assess your success with specific goals. Setting a target of consuming five fruits and vegetables five days a week, for example, is better than a general goal of' eating more vegetables.' You are less likely to feel stressed and then give up.

- **Reward yourself**: When you reach your goal, celebrate your new behaviour and performance for a few days, and then consider setting your next target.

- **Set Applicable Goals**: Objectives should apply to your life and career path. By having expectations consistent with this, you can grow your concentration and do what you want. Set goals that are common and contradictory, and you're going to squeeze away your time – and your future.

7.3 Prepare for slip-ups

Trying to change a pattern, you go along well for a while, and then have a relapse. It is perfectly normal. Once they reach their goals, many people try and try again.

What are the things that could cause a setback? If you've never tried to change a pattern, think about what has motivated you and what's in the way. Plan by learning about these hurdles now, and how to tackle them if they happen.

There will be a time when you're going to slip up and not make your weekly goal. Don't get frustrated when this happens. Learn from the experience. Ask yourself what's in the way of achieving your goal. When you make lifestyle changes, positive thinking goes a long way.

Stop negative thinking: The more lifestyle changes you have, the easier it is to make those changes.

Seek help with these tips:

- Find a friend: It's motivating to know that another individual also wants to change their lifestyle in the same way, like being more active or altering their eating habits. You've got someone who counts on you to help him, or he succeeds you can remind the person how far they – and you - have come.

- Involve your friends and family: They can work with or encourage you by telling you how they admire what you are doing. With your new healthy eating effort, family members will join in. Don't be afraid to tell your family and friends that their support can make a big difference for you.

- Join a support group or class: Some of the same obstacles plague people in these communities. If you don't feel like sticking to your strategy, they will give you help. When you need a lift, they boost your morale. You can find many support groups online.

- Reinforce yourself positively: Do not waste time feeling bad about yourself when you feel like giving up. Consider why you want to improve, about the strides you've made, and give yourself a pep talk, a pat on the back and a hug.

- Get professional assistance: A registered dietician will help you make healthy choices while still encouraging you to eat the food you love. A trainer or physiotherapist can develop an enjoyable and easy-to-stay exercise program. Your family physician, counsellor, or a social worker will help you to resolve obstacles, reduce stress, or stop smoking.

Healthy eating

Get help when you change your eating habits, so you've chosen to change your eating habits. Good! Have you considered getting support to make this change?

It is an essential part of change to have the support of the people closest to you. If you change careers, a routine, or how you eat doesn't matter as support gives you a better chance to make the change work.

Many people can provide support. Your family and friends can influence the way you eat, but you can also get help from others. There are many types of assistance. Remaining on track can be motivated by constructive words and actions or gentle reminders.

Research shows that it is essential to get support from spouses, family members, and friends to make behavioural changes that affect health. Some people you may expect to support may not help you and may even make it more difficult for you to succeed.

You will determine with whom you would like to discuss your change plans.

- How can you help your family and friends?

- Your family and friends can help you a lot to change the way you live, but you need to discuss it with them.

- Tell your family and friends why this move is being made. Give them reasons and explain why they matter to you.

- Tell them you want their support, but don't expect them to change their lives for you. If they're going to make some of the same improvements in food as you are, it's perfect. But even without changing the way they feed, they will help you.

Here are a few steps that you and your family can do together for better eating:

- Maintain a regular meal schedule for the family. Families who eat meals together regularly tend to eat healthier foods and stay closer to a healthier weight than those who do not.

- You may be able to discuss some of the same eating changes with your family. This may entail compromise on the part of everybody. It may mean fewer foods and more from others.

- If your diet is different from what your family eats, ask them to eat meals once a week from your food plan. If they see this as pleasant as the food they normally eat, they may choose to eat more of what you choose.

- Installation of a 'no food' policy. Make a food-free room. You can use this space to do stuff you might have done when eating in the kitchen, such as paying bills or helping children with homework. Staying out of the kitchen will help you stick with your food schedule.

- Remove stuff you don't want to consume and place it out of reach. When they have finished eating, remind family members not to leave food on the table.

- Set up a kitchen or refrigerator shelf for healthy foods only. You're going to want several healthy choices when you're hungry.

- Explain the new habit to your children. When you take the kids out once a week for pizza, should you then make a healthier pizza at home? Or you might go out to eat but order the pizza with a salad and other healthy foods. This allows you to fill in other foods in order to eat fewer pizza slices. See if you can find something that everyone can agree on.

- Get support from your friends and family. Ask them not to say negative things about you or what you eat.

- Celebrate with you when you achieve your goals. Take a cooking class or else go to the movies together. Keep reminding yourself and others that you're right.

- To help you make healthy food choices. For example, tell them to help you to eat more fruits and vegetables,

- Encourage you as you slip away from your eating plan. A reminder of how well you have done will help you get back on plan.

- Respect your new habits and they will not urge you to eat foods you don't want to eat.

Most people find that having a friend or food buddy makes the transition easier. A food buddy is someone who is also making changes in his or her eating habits. Learning that someone has the same goals is motivating. Your girlfriend can remind you how far you have come to support you when you have a hard time following your eating plan. For starters, you and your buddy will chat about healthy recipes, ways to prepare regular meals, and how to integrate small amounts of your favourite foods into the food plan.

You may think that friends or family members are doing things that make you feel bad. They don't seem to want you to be good. They may force you to eat more than you like, comment negatively on your new eating habits, and point out how many times you may have messed up.

If this happens, talking to these people is essential. They may not know they're doing it, or that it's upsetting you. Ask them to stop doing it if you need to. You can also ask them why they behave like this. You may find that they are worried that they will be left out or that you will make them look bad. They may not like the publicity you gain from your change.

If you've decided to start a healthy eating program, making that decision is a significant step towards becoming a healthier person.

Keep these essential points in mind:

- Whether it's healthy eating, getting more exercise, or quitting smoking, you have a better chance of success if you plan ahead.

- Understanding why you want to eat healthier will help your eating habits improve. And if you get discouraged, writing down your reasons will be a good reminder later.

- A plan to develop new habits includes long- and short-term goals as well as strategies to resolve barriers - things that may impede your progress.

- Start with small, short-term goals you can easily reach. Staying with something desired is simpler if you have early, regular achievements.

- Family and friends' encouragement can go a long way to help you achieve healthier eating success. Let them know what you're trying to do and why you are asking for their help.

How are you going to start a healthy eating plan?

It's necessary not to leap in too quickly. You will be ready for success with gradual, steady steps. You will learn the steps to follow in setting up a healthy eating plan:

- Set your goals

- Monitor your development

- Remember the obstacles

- Get help from others and yourself

It's time to set your goals when you're clear about your reasons for beginning a healthy eating program. What is your target for the long term?

You want to reach a long-term goal in 6 to 12 months.

Decreasing your blood pressure and/or cholesterol, for example, maybe your long-term goal or reaching a healthy body weight. What are the short-term priorities that are going to get you get there? Short-term goals are things you'd like to do tomorrow and the next day. For example, you may decide to take a low-fat or skim milk or soy beverage instead of whole milk on your cereal to reduce your intake of fat. Or eat fast food once a week or red meat only two times a week.

Some quick tips on healthy eating goals:

- Change your diet plan overnight; instead make your improvements one at a time.

- Instead of taking something away, add something to your diet. Add foods like fruits and vegetables; you need more. You might feel deprived if you start by taking things out of your diet, like foods high in fat or sugar. That will make change more difficult for you.

- Choose more healthy foods you're enjoying. Make a list of the foods you want and see how to make them healthier. For example, use low-fat mozzarella cheese and lots of fresh vegetables to make pizza at home. Do you like a particular raw plant? Stock up on it and reach for it every time you want a snack.

- Write down and hang your goals where you can see them. It can be a helpful reminder to reread your intentions.

- Do not set targets for fast weight loss. Sudden weight loss is not safe, and it is challenging to continue to do.

- Keeping track of your success lets you see how far you have come. It allows you to stick with your strategy as well. Use a diary, log, or food record form to chart the healthy things you're doing. Look at them when you start to doubt or feel discouraged.

Be careful about how you behave. When you eat better, do you notice any difference? Or do you see any difference in eating poorly at times?

Note whether your food preferences are shifting. We learn to like new foods as we change what we consume. You may find that you don't want to eat some of the foods you used to eat before you started making dietary changes. And you might have learned to like new foods you didn't think you wanted.

Take a look at any laboratory tests you may have after you adopted a special diet. You may see changes. Blood sugar checks will tell you if your diet has helped regulate your diabetes. Annual blood tests can assess cholesterol and triglyceride levels.

You should test your blood pressure to see if dietary changes are making it better. If you have high blood pressure, check your blood pressure at home. Reward yourself when you meet your target.

Think about the obstacles. Take your time to think about what might hinder your success. We name these barriers. And by learning about them now, if they happen, you can plan on how to manage them.

Some tips for overcoming barriers:

- Doing something, stopping it, and then getting mad at yourself is perfectly normal. Once they reach their goals, many people have to try and try again.

- Don't forget little bonuses, something to look forward to keep you going.

- Expect obstacles to be identified. And remember that the goal is not to remove barriers, but to identify them in advance and prepare what you are going to do to overcome them.

- It may help to have a written personal action plan listing your goals, obstacles, and strategies to resolve those barriers.

And get support - from others and yourself. It will be easier to change your eating habits, the more help you have. If your family members tell you they love how healthy you are, you're going to be motivated to keep up the excellent job.

And out there's more help. You can even ask for incentives. Looking for a few things: don't forget to repay yourself. Give yourself a treat when you hit one of your targets - eating five portions of fruits and vegetables a day for one week, for example.

Purchase a safe cookbook for yourself. Take a class of cooking. Or just take yourself a little time. Do everything it takes to reassure yourself that your targets have been achieved. You have reached it!

Hack 6- Implementation and Measuring

Be creative while inventing ideas, but be disciplined while implementing them - Amit Kalantri

Chapter 8

Stack Your Goals

Evidence has shown that if you make a specific plan for when, where, and how you execute an action, you are two to three times more likely to stick to your goals. For example, in a study, scientists asked people to address this sentence: 'I will engage in at least 25 minutes of vigorous exercise on [DAY] at [TIME OF DAY] at/in [PLACE] during the next week.' Researchers found that individuals who filled out this sentence were more likely to exercise as compared to that group that did not make plans for their future behaviour. Psychologists call these specific plans 'implementation expectations' as they specify when, where, and how a particular activity is to be enforced. This result have been replicated across hundreds of studies. It has shown to increase the chances that people will continue to exercise, start recycling, stick with learning, and even stop smoking.

The best way to use this finding is adopt or stack the habit of a strategy call. To use habit stacking, simply fill in this phrase: for example, I will

[NEW HABIT] after / Before [CURRENT HABIT].

Here are some examples:

• Meditation: I'm going to meditate for a minute after I brew my morning coffee.

• Push-ups: I'm going to do ten push-ups before taking my morning shower.

• Flossing: I'm going to floss my teeth after I put my toothbrush down.

• Gratitude: I'm going to say one thing I'm thankful for before I eat dinner.

• Networking: I will send an email to someone after I get back from my lunch break.

Habit stacking works well because you're not only making a specific plan for when and where to achieve your goals, but you're also linking your new goals to something you're doing every day. Researchers think this is a useful way of bridging the gap between goals and systems. The goals tell us what we want to do while the mechanism we implement every day is the process. Habit stacking and executing goals help us move to the specific process that will make the target in our heads a reality.

8.1 Set the Upper Bound

We almost always concentrate on the lower bound when we set goals. I'm speaking of the minimum threshold we're going to hit. The implicit assumption is, 'Yeah, if you can do more than the minimum, go for it.'

• An individual may say, 'This month, I want to lose at least 5 pounds.'

• An entrepreneur might say, 'Today, I want to make at least ten sales calls.'

• An author could say, 'Today, I want to write at least 500 words.'

• A basketball player could say, 'Today, I want at least 50 free throws.'

You could say:

• 'I want to lose at least 5 pounds this month, but not more than 10.'

• 'I want to make at least 10 sales calls today, but not more than 20.'

• 'I want to write at least 500 words today, but not more than 1,500.'

•' I want to make at least 50 free throws today, but not more than 100.'

To make progress, you want to push hard enough, but not so much that it is unsustainable. This is where it may be beneficial to set an upper limit. Upper limits make it simpler for you to keep up with your success.

In the beginning, this is particularly critical. The most significant thing is to show up anytime you set a new target and start working towards it. At first, showing up is even more important than succeeding because if you don't develop the habit of showing up, then in the future, you will never have anything to change.

How to achieve your Goals consistently

Good goal setting allows the structure that surrounds us to be addressed. Too often, within the wrong system, we set the right goals. If we fight the order every day to make progress, then making consistent progress will be hard.

There are all sorts of hidden forces that make it easier or more challenging to achieve our goals. Our worlds must be consistent with our goals.

8.2 How to Align Your Environment with Your Goals

While most of us at any given time have the freedom to make a broad range of choices, we sometimes make decisions based on the world in which we find ourselves. For instance, if you wanted to write a guide, you might drink a beer. You could be sitting at your desk with a glass of water next to you, though. No beers in sight. While you can get up, walk to the car, drive to the supermarket, and buy a beer, you probably won't because easier alternatives surround you. In this situation, the default decision is to take a sip of water - an easy decision.

Similarly, the choices that surround us form many of the decisions we make in our professional and personal lives. When you sleep with your phone next to your pillow, the default decision is likely to check social media and emails as soon as you wake up.

When you step into your living room, and all of your couches and chairs are facing the TV, watching the screen is possibly the default choice.

When you have alcohol in your house, the default choice is to drink regularly.

Defaults can also be optimistic, of course. When you have a dumbbell next to your desk at work, it is more likely to be the default choice to churn out some fast curls. When you carry a water bottle with you throughout the day, the default option is more likely to be drinking water rather than soda. When you put floss in a visible location (like your toothbrush), the default choice is more likely to be flossing.

Scientists refer to the effect that defaults on the world can have as the architecture of choice on decision-making. This has a significant impact on achieving goals. Whether or not you reach your long-term goals has a lot to do with what kinds of forces surround you in the moment. In a negative environment, it is tough to stick to good behaviours.

Here are a few strategies that I found useful in for life when trying to design better default decisions for simplicity. When you are constantly surrounded by noise, it's hard to focus on the signal. If the kitchen is filled with junk food, it is harder to eat well. When you have ten tabs open in your desktop window, it's harder to concentrate on reading a blog post. If you slip into the illusion of multitasking, it is harder to accomplish the most crucial task. Eliminate the choices in question.

Placing products on eye-level shelves in the store makes them more recognisable and more likely to be purchased. You can use visual signals like the Paper Clip System or the Seinfeld Strategy outside the store to create an environment that subtly nudges the acts in the right direction.

Opt-out or opt-in.

There is a modern study of organ donation that showed how many European countries have skyrocketed their rates of organ donation: they wanted people to opt-out of donation rather than opt-in. In your life, you can do something similar by choosing your future self ahead of time through better habits. For example, you might schedule your next week's yoga session when you feel motivated today. You have to justify opting-out instead of motivating yourself to opt-in when your workout rolls around.

8.3 Measure Your Goals

Measurement is another secret to the long-term success of your goals. The human mind is fond of receiving feedback. Proof of success is one of the most inspiring things we can encounter. That's why measurement is so critical to setting goals effectively. You gain insight into whether or not you are making progress by evaluating performance. The things we are measuring are those we are improving. If we get better or worse, it is only through numbers and simple monitoring that we have some idea.

Here are some of the measurable goals:

I got stronger when I measured how many pushups I've made.

I read more books while I recorded my 20-page reading habit a day.

I started to live with more integrity when I recorded my values.

The trick is to understand that it is not specifically about the outcome to count, weigh, and track. Moreover, it is a means of learning, finding out, and knowing. Test to see if you're present. Check to see if the things that are important to you are spending time.

8.3 Measure Backward, Not Forward

When looking ahead, you measure progress. You're setting goals. For success, you schedule milestones. Ultimately, to some extent, you are trying to predict the future.

In industry, wellness, and life as a whole, ask this.

- Is it possible to increase your quarterly earnings by 20%?

- In the next three months, will you lose 20 pounds?

- Going to be married at 30?

These are all forward-looking calculations. You're looking ahead trying to guess when you're going to get somewhere. There's a different approach, and more useful: calculate backwards, not forward.

Measuring backward vs measuring forward

Sit down at your computer every week and fill out a little spreadsheet to chart your business' critical metrics: traffic, subscribers to email, sales, expenditures, etc. By now, you've been down the road pretty often, so it only takes about 15 minutes.

However, you get straightforward input in those 15 minutes as to whether or not you are making progress in the areas that matter most. You can tell the way things are moving. And, if the numbers shift the wrong way in one week, the following week, you can make adjustments.

Essentially, you calculate backward progress (what happened this week in your business?) and use back calculation as a way to direct your next week's acts. In the gym, you can use a similar strategy: each Tuesday, Thursday, and every Friday, open your journal when you arrive to look at the weights you lifted during your last or two workouts. So, by marginally increasing the sets, reps, or weight from where they were from last week, you schedule your workout. Of course, you are looking for small increases. You are interested in the return of one percent.

You calculate backwards in the gym, just like in your company, and use that calculation to decide your next move. You are still looking for improvement, but you base your decisions on what has happened recently, not on what you think will happen in the future.

The habit chains are too weak to feel until they are too strong to be broken.

Samuel Johnson said one of our greatest struggles is to keep aware of what we are doing when it comes to building good habits and breaking bad habits. The more a behaviour becomes automatic, the less likely it is to be noticed. This helps to explain how we can be sneaked into the consequences of bad habits. By the time we consider the consequences of our decisions, we are already dependent on the new behaviour pattern.

Measuring backwards, however, will draw attention to these unseen patterns by making you conscious of what you are doing. Measuring backwards allows you to consider your recent actions. You can't live in a world of hopes and dreams like in a fairy tale. You need to look at what has happened recently in your life and then base your choices and changes on these data bits.

The news is that you can make your decisions on what you are currently doing, not on what you are hoping to do for your future self.

The importance of short-term feedback

'The best way to improve long-term behaviour is with short-term feedback.' —Seth Godin. This approach has one caveat: the data needs to come from the recent past when you calculate backwards.

If you used data to assess progress and make business decisions two years ago, your choices would have been off. The same applies to weightlifting or other areas of improvement. You don't want decisions to be focused on what you have done long ago, but on what you've recently achieved. In other words, you want to input in the short term, not in the long term - the better, the quicker.

Measuring for satisfaction

This approach has an additional benefit. When you calculate backwards, you will be able to enjoy the change you are making now rather than looking forward to a new life in the future.

Once you hit a potential milestone or goal, you don't have to put off your joy. Happiness in the future is no longer the endgame out there. Focusing on how you can improve your past self in the immediate future is more satisfying than comparing your current state to where you hope to be someday.

Put the idea into practice

Almost every improvement you want to make in your life requires some kind of change in behaviour. You have to do something differently if you want different results. The hard question to answer is, what are you expected to do differently to get the results you want?

You tend to react by focusing on an outcome and setting a target. Goals are excellent, and it's essential to have a sense of direction to where you want to go. Yet calculating backwards is the way to go when it comes to determining the changes you can make right now. Let the recent results guide your actions in the future. For example:

Weight loss: test your intake of calories. Last week, did you eat 3,500 calories a day? Based this week, on an average of 3,400 per day

Strength Training: well, you squatted 250 pounds last week for five sets of 5 reps? Give this week a try of 255 pounds.

Relationships: last week, how many new people have you met? If zero, then reflect on this week's introduction to a new individual.

Entrepreneurship: although your average is five, you landed just two customers last week? It sounds like this week; you're going to focus on making further sales calls.

Measure backwards and get a bit better afterwards. What have you been doing last week? How can you change this week just a bit?

8.4 The Seinfeld Strategy

Seinfeld said the way to be a better comic is to create better jokes and the way to create better jokes is to write jokes every day. He got a big wall calendar and hung it on the wall for a whole year. A big red magic marker was his next move. He said, '[I'll do my writing assignment for every day; I'll put a big red X over that day.'

You're going to have a chain after a few days. Just hold on to it, and every day the chain will grow longer. You'll love to see that chain, especially if you get under your belt for a couple of weeks. Your only duty is not to break the chain.

You will notice that Seinfeld hasn't said a single result thing. Whether he was inspired or not, it didn't matter. It didn't matter whether or not he wrote great jokes. It didn't matter if it ever make it into a series he was working on. And that's one of the clear truths behind the incredible success and continuity of Seinfeld.

How to stop procrastinating by using the Seinfeld Method

Top performers in all sectors - athletes, singers, CEOs, artists - are all more reliable than their peers. Day after day, they wake up and deliver while everyone else gets stuck with the urgencies of everyday life and fights a constant battle between procrastination and motivation.

While most people get demotivated and off-track after a poor performance, a bad workout, or just a bad day at work, the next day, top performers settle back into their routine.

The Seinfeld Strategy works because it helps to shift focus away from each performance and puts emphasis on the process. It's not about how you look, how motivated you are, or the beauty of that day's work. Instead, it's just about 'not breaking the chain.' All you have to do is pick up a calendar and launch your chain to apply this technique to your own life.

A Word of Note

The Seinfeld Strategy has one drawback. You have to choose a job important enough to make a difference, but it's easy enough to get it completed. If you could write ten pages a day for your book, it would be great, but it's not a sustainable chain to create. Likewise, in theory, it sounds great to be able to raise the dead like a man every day, but in reality, you are likely to be overstrained and burned out.

Step one is, therefore, to choose a job that is sufficiently easy to be sustainable. At the same time, you must ensure that your acts are sufficiently relevant to the matter.

Looking for good jokes every day, for example, is easy, but you will never write a joke just by researching. This is why the writing process is a better choice. Writing, even when performed in small doses, will produce a meaningful result.

Likewise, it could be useful and straightforward to do ten pushups per day, depending on your fitness level. It will make you stronger. Moreover, it's simple to read a fitness book every day, but it won't get you in better shape.

Pick tasks that are easy to maintain and capable of achieving the desired outcome. Another way of saying this is to focus on actions and not motions. Consider the concept: mistakes smart people master follow consistency.

The central question that binds our community together - and what you are trying to write about every Monday and Thursday - is, 'How do you live a healthy life?' It involves not just nutrition and exercise, but discovery and adventure, art and imagination, and culture and connection.

But they all need consistency, no matter what topic you are talking about. No matter what your definition of a 'healthy life' is, to make it a reality, you will have to fight procrastination. Ideally, the Seinfeld Strategy will help bring this war into perspective.

Don't break your exercise chain, and you'll quickly find that you're getting fit. Don't split the business chain, and you're going to find the results are coming much quicker. Do not break the chain of your artistic pursuits, and you will find that you are continually generating creative work.

Believe that success takes a monumental effort and that your lofty goals require enormous amounts of determination and inspiration. Al you need is to commit yourselves to small, manageable tasks. Mastery is the result of consistency.

8.5 Why and How to Track Ultimate Habit Tracking

Maintaining a habit tracking is one easy and useful thing you can do if you want to stick to a habit for good. Here's why: top performers also chart their success, measure it, and report it in different ways. Every small calculation enables feedback. It sends a signal as to whether progress is being made or whether changing direction is required.

Gabrielle Hamilton, a New York City chef, is a good example. During an interview, she said, 'The one thing I see is that the chef is constantly separated from the home cook is that we taste everything, all the time, right down to the salt grains, before we apply it to the pan. We slurp olive oil glasses and aerate them in our mouths as if it was a wine that we tried to know.'

The Habit Tracker: what is it and how does it works

A habit tracker is an easy way to measure if you've made a habit. The most basic method is to get a calendar and stick to your schedule every day. For instance, if you meditate on Monday, Wednesday, and Friday, you get an X for each of those dates. The calendar will become a record of your habit streak as time goes by.

Develop a Habit Journal containing twelve habit tracker templates, one for each month to make this process as easy as possible. All you need to do is add your habit and start to cross off the days.

The classic approach is to put an X on each day. If you are a little more design-oriented, on your habit tracker, you can shade in the cells. You can also use checkmarks or fill your habit tracker with dots. The key point here is that your habit tracker gives clear evidence that you have achieved the habit. It's a symptom that progress is being made. Of course, that's not all it does.

There are three reasons why habit tracking is strong:

- It provides a visual cue for you to act.

- Seeing the progress you are making is inspiring. You don't want your string to end.

- Recording your success at the moment feels rewarding.

Let's break down every single one.

Advantage #1: You are prompted to behave by a habit tracker.

Naturally, habit tracking builds a series of visual indications. You'll be reminded to act again when you look at the calendar and see your streak.

Studies have shown that people who monitor their progress on goals such as weight loss, smoking cessation, and lowering blood pressure are all more likely to increase success than those that don't. A survey of over 1600 people found that those who maintained a daily food log lost twice weight as those who did not. A habit tracker is a simple way of recording your actions and monitoring a pattern that will trigger the urge to change it.

Tracking your habits keeps you accountable, as well. Most of us say that we are doing better than others. Measurement offers one way of overcoming our blindness to our behaviour and noticing what's going on every day. You will not lie to yourself when the evidence is right in front of you.

Advantage #2: You are encouraged to proceed with a habit tracker.

Progress is the most effective motivation. We become more motivated to continue to the path when we get a signal that we are moving forward. Tracking habits can have an addictive impact on motivation in this way: every little victory feeds your desire.

On a bad day, this can be especially powerful. When you're feeling down, all the progress you've already made is easy to forget. Tracking your habit offers visual evidence of your hard work and a subtle reminder of how far you have come. Plus, the empty square you see every morning will motivate you to get started because by breaking your streak, you don't want to lose your progress.

Advantage #3: A habit tracker gives instant gratification.

Eventually, it is easy to watch. Crossing an item off your to-do list, completing an entry in your workout log, or marking an X on the calendar is satisfactory. Watching your performance grow is good, and you are more likely to survive.

Habit monitoring also helps keep your eye on the ball: you focus more on the system than on the result. You're not going to get six-pack abs; you're just trying to keep the streak alive and become the type of person who does not skip workouts.

Ideas and benefits sound great, but you don't have to fill your habit tracker with any habits that make up your day. Yes, if you're already sticking to a routine, then monitoring it as well seems like extra work. So what is your habit tracker going to measure?

Habit monitoring will help you set off a new habit or keep track of habits you tend to forget or slip when things get busy. It is recommended to use the Two-Minute Rule from Atomic Behaviours, which recommends you scale down your behaviours until two minutes or fewer are required to execute them. You can log whatever habits you want in your habit tracker, but it is suggested to start with these super-small habits to make sure you show up every day, at least in a small way.

See the examples below and split them out into daily, weekly, and monthly patterns.

A widespread daily habit of tracking:

- journal one sentence
- one minute push up
- stretch for one minute
- write one thing that makes me happy
- make the bed

- wake up by [TIME]

- go to bed by [TIME]

- take a shower

- floss my teeth

- weigh myself

- take medication

- take vitamins/supplements

- play [INSTRUMENT] for one minute

- touch one potential customer

- prioritize my to-do list

- say 'I love you' at least once

- put all the dishes away

- take a walk

- call mother

- walk the dog

Note that most things on this list take a minimum of one minute to two. Make your habits so easy that even on the tough days, you can stick to them.

You need to repeat the list frequently to make something genuinely habitual. As a result, the bulk of activities are every day. But using a habit tracker for different weekly or monthly routines can also be helpful. Behaviours, like tying your shoes or brushing your teeth, will not become 'automatic,' but a habit tracker can still remind you to complete them.

Popular weekly habits to track:
- publish a blog post
- vacuum
- take out the trash/do recycling
- do laundry
- water plants
- clean up bedroom
- write a thank-you note
- check finances
- transfer money to savings account
- pay off credit cards
- pay deep clean house bills

You can also use a habit tracker to count how often you do something simple. For instance, you may want to keep track of how many days you travel each month for work. Consider.

- days spent travelling

- perform daily reviews

- perform monthly reviews

You can use a behaviour tracker to monitor what you are not doing. These are called 'evasion patterns' (that is, activities that you try to avoid). See our website for free downloadable resources

Good new habits:

- no alcohol

- no Netflix

- no buying online

- no soda

- no sugar

- no caffeine

- no smoking

The Habit Journal provides a proven template and the fastest way to create your habit tracker. No need to draw your grid for an hour. Simply write down your routines, and you're good to go.

Get used to using your Habit Tracker

With all the advantages of using a habit tracker, however, it isn't something that makes sense in every circumstance or for individual. Many people oppose the notion of monitoring and measuring. It may feel like a challenge because it pushes you into two habits: the habit you try to build and the habit of observing it. That said, almost anyone in one way or another can benefit from habit tracking, even if it is only temporary.

Can we do to make it easier to track habits?

The most critical activities should be limited to manual monitoring. It is easier to track one habit continuously than to track ten sporadically. Keep your habit tracker easy and limit it to three or four major habits.

Immediately after the habit occurs, record the calculation. The habit's completion is the prerequisite to writing it down. (This is a variation on the 'habit piling' strategy. Here's the basic formula: I'll [TRACK MY HABIT] after [CURRENT HABIT].

For example:

- mark the column 'call one potential client' after hanging up the phone from a sales call.

- fill the column 'meditate for one minute' after you finish meditating.

- After putting your plate in the dishwasher, finish the line 'clean all the dishes.'

The practice of using the habit tracker is what we're talking about here. These little rules will help you remember to pick up your habit tracker and mark another achievement.

Quick recovery when your habits break down

Finally, when you fall off the wagon at some point, every habit strike stops. Perfection cannot be accomplished. An emergency is coming up soon: you get sick, or you have to travel for work, or your family needs a little more time. Try to remind yourself of a simple rule when this happens: never miss it twice.

Hack 7- Meditation

Meditation is a process of lightening up, of trusting the basic goodness of what we have and who we are, and of realizing that any wisdom that exists in what we already have. The key is to wake up, to become more alert, more interested and curious about ourselves

- Pema Chodron

Chapter 9

Habitual patterns limit our options and hold us hostage. Our thoughts and emotions default to a usual response due to the tendencies we create out of habit. Without awareness, we dig into our minds ever deeper grooves: habitual behaviour patterns that can either be positive or negative. Through the practice of awareness, we can start to see this process and disrupt it over time.

It can be present for just one moment every time we have thought that arises and goes by, or we can repeat it to ourselves over and over again. For me, it's like water; it can go anywhere if you pour a drop on the earth. But if that drop begins to take some path, and the next drops follow, the water will make a groove after a while.

Each time a drop goes down that path, it creates a deeper rhythm, and the choices are becoming increasingly limited. Meditation awareness leads to more mental freedom; the knowledge we gain in meditation is a way to get us back to square one, where the water now has options to flow.

Consciousness is the key to solving the issues that our normal responses bring. Let's take recurring fears as an example. We may have been in or witnessed a car accident, so we react in some way whenever we think of a 'car.' And every time we have this reaction, we intensify the rhythm so that we have the same reaction the next time the stimulus occurs. But with awareness, we understand what is happening at the moment so that each time an event happens, new knowledge is generated. Every time we get a little faster understanding.

Eventually, the very moment it arises, we find ourselves recognizing our usual tendency. This is the moment we have different possibilities. The water doesn't have to go down the same channel because we're at a place where different ways can steer a dropping drop. We know that we've got options. The deeper our practice of mindfulness, the greater our independence and ability to understand and work with our impulses.

We can apply this practice to the usual tendencies with family members, difficult co-workers, etc. that always seem to abound. Typically, our leanings determine our reactions because we don't know about them and often capture them too late – if at all. We've been swept away without awareness, since we've already reacted. Everything was going too fast; we didn't catch it in time. But with awareness, the moment it manifests, we can see our tendency and change our response to something more workable, and more beneficial. The ideal technique is meditation. If we develop the powerful habit of returning to the breath in meditation when something occurs midstream, we keep our awareness in all kinds of situations. We've disrupted the usual pattern, and now the water has a new place to go.

Events get out of control when certain factors are present. And it's just because of the knowledge that things are dwindling back to normal. They are falling back into proportion, and with what is going on, we can have a more balanced and healthy relationship. We are also cultivating a kind of trust in resting with the breath, along with awareness. Try it and see for yourself the subtle changes it makes. You can keep it in your pocket once you've had the experience and use it when you're in a usual 'trigger' situation.

It doesn't only happen on the cushion

Meditation is not something that only happens on the cushion. When we're sitting, there's awareness, focus, and presence; but there's no reason they can't be there every moment of your life. When intense situations happen and create fear, anxiety, or conflict, you're usually likely to be swept away. But actually, because it's such an intense experience, and so in your face, tagging it and reacting differently is easier for you!

Subtle thoughts and worries are equally bad habits, and they are harder to work with because they appear to be hidden. You don't see them since it's the big things that bring you back to your preparation and remind you that you can use this device, this gift, or good practice to improve your experience. When you change your experience, you change the entire situation effectively. It may not be 100 percent of the time, but because you are aware, your reactions can potentially be more measured and healthier. Between behaving with indifference and acting with knowledge, there is a vast difference

Steps for meditation

1. Sit comfortably on a chair, your feet on the floor, and your hands on your thighs. (You can sit on the floor if you prefer.) Take two or three deep breaths and close your eyes.

2. Starting from the top of your head and moving down, scan your body mentally, noticing any tension in your muscles, places of comfort or discomfort, while feeling the floor under your

feet. Start paying attention to your breath's natural rhythm.

3. Follow the rising and falling sensation without changing it in any way, silently counting breaths as you become more conscious of your breath.

Inevitably, your mind will wander. This is one of the first lessons of meditation. When you notice that you've been distracted by a thought, let go of it and give your attention back to your breath. You're going to learn to step back over time and just watch the views. The same applies to sounds: let them come and go instead of trying to block them out.

4. Take a few seconds to allow your mind to do whatever it wants. (You may find your mind is tranquil.) Realizing the sounds around you and putting your attention back to the body, slowly open your eyes.

When to do it: many people meditate the first thing in the morning, to start the day with a clear head, but everybody's different, so find what works for you.

How often: the more you practice, the sooner you will see benefits, but consistency matters more than quantity, so concentrate on 'small and often,' taking the time to build a strong base. If every day sounds like too much at first, continue with three to five days a week.

How long: for beginners, just ten minutes a day will suffice. (Use a timer or an app, so you didn't have to watch the clock.) For some people that has always been enough, but ultimately you may decide to sit for more extended periods, especially once you begin to feel the wonderfulness of your newfound headspace.

Tricks to Make New Habits Stick

Creating better jokes was the way to be a better comedian, so write better jokes every day - Seinfeld

Chapter 10

Pick up a big wall calendar and hang it all year round on a common wall. The next pass was a big red magic marker. Seinfeld said that daily I'm going to do my writing assignment; every day, I'm going to put a big red X.

You're going to have a chain after a couple of days. Just hang on to it, and the chain will grow longer every day. You're going to love seeing that chain, particularly if you get under your belt for a couple of weeks. Your effort is not to break the chain.

It didn't matter if he was inspired or not. Whether or not he wrote great jokes didn't matter. If he ever turned it into a collection of what he was working on, it didn't matter.

And this is one of the simple facts behind Seinfeld's incredible success and continuity.

Let's talk about not procrastinating in your life using the Seinfeld Process

How to avoid procrastinating

Top performers in all fields - athletes, actors, CEOs, musicians - are all more efficient than their peers. They get up and deliver day after day while everyone else gets stuck with daily life's urgencies and fights a constant battle among procrastination and motivation.

Most people get demotivated and off-track due to poor performance, a bad workout, or just a bad day at work, top performers settle back into their routine the next day. The Seinfeld Strategy works because it helps shift focus away from every event and focuses on the process. It's not about how you look, how you're motivated, or the beauty of the work of that day.

You have to pick up a calendar and start your chain to apply this technique to your own life.

A word of note

One drawback to the Seinfeld Strategy. You have to choose work sufficiently important to make a difference, but simple enough to complete . It would be great if you could write ten pages a day for your book, but it's not a sustainable chain. Likewise, it sounds great in theory to be able to raise the dead like a man every day, but you're likely to be overstrained and burned out.

Thus, step one is to choose a career that is easy to sustain. At that time, you have to make sure your actions are important enough to matter. For example, it's easy to look for good jokes every day, but you're never going to write a joke just by researching. That's why it is a better choice to write. Writing will produce a meaningful result, even if done in small doses.

Depending on your fitness level, it could also be easy and useful to do ten pushups a day. It's going to make you happier. It's also easy to read every day a fitness novel, but it won't get you in better shape.

Choose tasks that are easy to maintain and able to achieve the desired result.

Another way to say this is to concentrate on acts rather than movements, which is the idea discussed in my article: Mistake That Smart People Make Mastery Follows Consistency.

The central question that ties our society together, and what I'm trying to write about every Monday and Thursday is, 'Where do you live a healthy life' But they all need to be consistent, regardless of the topic we are addressing. Regardless of what your idea of normal life is, you'll have to fight procrastination to make it a reality. Ideally, this conflict will be put into perspective by the Seinfeld Strategy.

Don't break the chain of exercise, and you'll soon find that you're getting fit. Don't break the company chain, and the results will come much quicker. Do not break the chain of your artistic pursuits, and you will find that creative work is continuously being produced.

So often, we conclude that success requires a monumental effort and that our lofty goals require a great deal of dedication and motivation. But all we need is to engage in small, manageable tasks. The result of consistency is mastery.

Maintaining a habit monitoring is one simple and useful thing you can do if you want to stick to a habit for good.

Here's why: top performers are also charting, calculating, and recording their performance in different ways. Every little measurement provides feedback. This sends a signal as to whether progress is being made or whether it is necessary to change direction.

A good example is Gabrielle Hamilton, a chef from New York City. She said during an interview with the New York Times, 'The one thing I see is that the chef is always isolated from the home cook is that we taste everything, all the time, right down to the salt grains, before adding it to the pan. We slurp olive oil glasses and aerate them in our mouths as if it were a wine we wanted to learn.'

10.1 How to Stick With Good Habits Every Day by Using the "Paper Clip Strategy"

Additional Tricks

A bank in Abbotsford, Canada hired a stockbroker named Trent Dyrsmid, a twenty-three years old, in 1993. Abbotsford was a relatively small suburb tucked in neighbouring Vancouver's shadow, where most of the big business deals were made. Nobody expected too much of him because of the position and the fact that Dyrsmid was a rookie. Yet, thanks to a simple daily routine, he made brisk progress.

The Paper Clip Strategy

Dyrsmid began with two jars on his desk every morning. One was loaded with 120 clips. The other was empty. He would make a sales call as soon as he settled in every day. He would move a paper clip from the full jar to the empty jar immediately afterwards, and the process would start again. 'I'd start with 120 paper clips in one jar every morning, and I'd keep dialling the phone until I moved all of them to the second jar,' he said.

Dyrsmid contributed $5 million to the organization within eighteen months. He made $75,000 a year by the age of twenty-four, the equivalent of $125,000 today. Not long after, he found another business with a six-figure salary.

The Tale of Trend: better habits that last vs habits that fail

When asked about his habit's specifics, Dyrsmid just said, I'd start calling at 8:00 a.m. Every day. He never looked at quotations from securities or analysis from analysts. He never read the newspaper all the time. If the news was relevant, it would reach him from other directions.

Dyrsmid is proof of a simple truth: success is often the result of constant dedication to the fundamentals. Compare Trent's results with where we often find you. We want our routines to be regular, but we're struggling to make it into the gym. What's the difference? While others break, why do some good habits stick? Why has the paper clip technique of Trent performed so well, and what can we learn from it?

The "Paper Clip Strategy" works particularly well with the Power of a Visual Flash because it provides a visual cue that helps motivate us to practice a behaviour more regularly. It is learned from writers who use it in a variety of ways. For example, as she wrote a page in her novel, one woman moved a hairpin from one jar to another. After every set of push-ups, another man moved a marble from one bin to the next.

It is rewarding to make progress, and visual steps such as moving paper clips or hairpins or marbles provide clear evidence of success. As a result, they improve our actions and bring to any task a little bit of immediate satisfaction.

Here are a few reasons why visual indicators work well to create new good habits. Visual indications encourage us to continue a practice. You lie about your ability to remember executing a new habit, like 'I'm going to start eating better. For real this time.' But, a few days later, the inspiration fades, and life's business begins to take over again. Making a new habit is usually a recipe for failure. That's why a visual stimulus can be so beneficial, like a bin full of paper clips. When your environment pushes you in the right direction, it's much easier to stick to good habits.

Physical signs show your improvement. Everybody recognizes that consistency is an essential component of success, but in fact, few people calculate how reliable they are in real life. The Paper Clip Strategy avoids this pitfall because it is an integrated measuring system. One look at your clips of paper and you have a sense of your success instantly.

Visual signs can have a motivational effect that is addictive It is normal to become more motivated to continue the habit as the visible evidence of progress mounts. The more paper clips you put in the jar, the more inspired you become to complete the task. Many current studies in behavioural economics refer to this as the Endowed Progress Effect, which essentially says that once you have them, you place more value on items. That is, the more paper clips you move to the 'completed' jar, the more valuable it becomes for you to complete the habit.

Physical cues can be used to boost motivation in the short and long term. The technique of the paper clip provides everyday inspiration, yet every day you start from scratch. Another form of visual cue, however, such as the 'don't break the chain' calendar mentioned, can be used to highlight the consistency over extended periods. You can create a set of visual signals by putting these two approaches together to inspire and monitor your patterns.

Creating your paper clip strategy

There are many ways to use the paper clip technique to accomplish goals. Would you like to do 100 pushups every day? Start with ten clips of paper and push one over each drop and do a set of 10 all day long.

Do you need to send 25 emails each day? Start with 25 clips, and each time you press 'Send', toss one to the other side.

Would you like to drink eight glasses of water every day? Start with 8 clips, and each time you finish a bottle, slide one over.

If you'd like to take a prescription three times a day, set 3 paper clips out each time you swallow your pills and drop one into the jar; it will cost you less than $10 for the entire strategy.

Take a box of standard paper clips. Choose two regular holders and start moving the bad guys from side to side. Trent Dyrsmid determined that one of his key tasks was to attain success in his field: making more calls for sales. He discovered that what makes the difference is to learn the fundamentals.

The same applies to your targets.

- There's no secret sauce

- There's no magic bullet
- The magic ingredient is good habits

10. 2 Make a Commitment to Your Self

It takes conscious thinking and planning to commit to forging good habits. In everything you do in life, either you honour your sacred self, or you don't. To achieve all this, there is a key step in transforming habits, preparing yourself mentally for a small action, and overcoming any obstacles thrown in your way.

'Do not concentrate on doing behaviour X. Rather, focus on making behaviour X easier to do.' Dr B.J. Fogg looked for ways to make the new habit easier to do. Each step of the new habit is for more nuanced changes and look for better ways to do it. Then see what might go wrong or kill you and think about ways to stop this happening.

Leaving the habit of smoking

Something like this can happen (after going through your addiction process and visualizing your higher purpose): you take out a favourite chewing gum from a little pocket with a zipper when you feel the cue for cigarettes.

Then you'll keep the gum in your mouth for 5 seconds and enjoy the minty taste before you start chewing. While doing this, you are going to close your eyes and play your positive quit smoking mental video.

Instead, while keeping your hands folded, you will start chewing slowly to avoid fidgeting. To avoid the situation of not getting a chewing gum, you must ensure that at all times, you have at least one pack in your purse or bag, one at home and one at the office. You are going to check every morning when you get ready to leave home and first thi9ng when you get to the office.

If you are having a smoking craving, you are going to excuse yourself and take a brisk 10-minute walk. Walk to energize yourself before you get back to work.

We make good habits stick when we commit ourselves. Because in everything we do in life, we value our spiritual selves, or don't. We must first find ourselves worthy of more and greater to achieve everything that lies in universal escrow.

So often in life, you introduce to other people your talents and resources. You make others a priority and you abandon yourself for the last time. The problem with this is when the rest of the world is 'pleased,' it's hardly time to look after who's most important, you.

Building good habits requires conscious thinking and planning. Whether it's increased exercise, more religious studies, learning, closer relationships, or perhaps healthier eating, it means setting aside time to decide what we like. We must permit ourselves to go after it when we know what it is.

Very often, we fell into the trap of knowing what we need, so we put it off for the future until 'the time is right.' It's always the right time! There's a saying, 'How it is now!' Make and go to your commitment!

Steps for sticking to habits

1. Be worthy: If you don't believe you're deserving of it, you won't ever manifest what you want out of life. Your worthiness rate is directly proportionate to what you can achieve. Understanding that you are as worthy as anybody else on this planet to accomplish your goals is vital to enter the process fully.

2. Consider your well-being a priority: This does not mean that we are disregarding our obligations. Maybe it's about encouraging others to be more worried about themselves rather than thinking we've got to do it all. There is a fine line in encouraging others to take on real responsibility.

3. Study your area of interest: There's so much data out there, and we can find almost any information we want with Google. We have already started to form your new habit by looking for your target. You're on the way! The acquisition of appropriate, sound information and knowledge about our targets will educate us in our areas of interest to begin to change our perceptions.

4. Be gentle with yourself: Like any significant change in life, we will sometimes slip back into old habits or lose track of our goals until they become a habit. It takes 30-45 days to create a new habit everywhere. Give a grace period to yourself as you work towards your goal. Missing a day, losing, or going off track is all right. We're more likely to stay in the old pattern if we beat ourselves up. Humanity's acceptance and grace will go a long way!

5. Pat on the back for a well-functioning job: Make yourself a cheerleader and motivational speaker. You know precisely what you need to do to keep going. Do not expect to receive praise from the outside world because somehow others appear to be short of what we need to hear because they come from their own projections.

Our life is our own. No one knows better what is going to nurture our souls and improve our lives than we do! Go for the dreams you have. You never know!

10.3 Start living from the more authentic, the more genuine within you

Most of us are worried about how we can better manage our lives by developing and maintaining better habits. However, the issue with the thinking about this is that you believe you can manage your life continuously discipline as the basic motivating principle.

You watch people apply this idea to their lives every only to see them, shortly afterwards, stop doing whatever they decided to do. Diets fail, exercise programs cease, lovers leave, and we go back and forth to the same old, tired arguments.

Why is it not working?

- You never like to be told what to do and
- You should try to apply Band-Aid to an old identity

Personality is the mask and costume you've been wearing since infancy that you donned from the expectations of your parent. You have become something but are not to remain attached to those you used to belong to. It's not that tag that you are. And at a certain time in your life, you begin to feel the difference between your true self and identity although you may not have the insight to see that this is what it is. You think one way, but you see something else.

You find that between what you want and what you think you have to do is conflicted thinking. A crisis makes you realize that you have lived a life that is not true to who you are. These are signals that you're beginning to wake up to who you are. To form behaviour patterns that satisfy you (i.e., good habits), you must start living the more authentic, more genuine you. The authentic self has its urges, desires, and living patterns, and it's all about wholeness. In the beginning, the task of discovering the authentic self is to hear; then live in its messages.

Cognitive-behavioural therapy: how to restructure CBT-related thoughts

Are your brain, thoughts, and habits unhelpful? Knowing this can assist cognitive behavioural therapy. Cognitive behavioural therapy is a form of psychotherapy that addresses problems and boosts happiness by modifying dysfunctional emotions, behaviours, and thoughts. Instead of deconstructing your childhood, cognitive behavioural therapy reconstructs new, adaptive thoughts to help you form useful habits. Such patterns will change your life's way of living, talking, and behaving. Think of CBT as a way to re-connect your brain. You can use CBT to transform unhelpful habits into effective habits.

Changing habits is not an easy task. There are three steps to changing habits:

1) Recognise what you want to improve and reflect on your behaviour. Identify the habit you want to replace with clear specificity and pay attention when it comes to it. This is being aware of it.

2) Focus on your behaviour when it comes to that habit or craving. Focus on bringing your mind to the habit with which you wish to replace it. Remember to focus on why you want to change or the advantages and disadvantages of acting on the urges. This will give you a very important 'why' to facilitate real change.

3) Purposeful repetition: Repetition is essential for developing new neural pathways in your brain. Stay conscious and purposeful in replacing the old habit with the new habit. Practice this action until it transforms into second nature.

Conclusion

Hacks to Change Habits in Thirty Days

You would only thrive as an early human if you had developed practical behaviours that kept you healthy and prosperous. To this end, your mind/body set new neural tracks automatically for whatever you repeatedly did.

Who would better feed his family: the hunter who stood his bow and arrow every night in the same place, or the one who got up every morning and had to search for them in the cave? Who would encourage her child to survive: the mother who regularly tested to see if she breastfed her baby or the one who did it erratically? Okay, you're getting the picture.

Here are five tips for building useful habits:

Tip #1: Intentionally, when comfortable, develop habits.

Practice specific ways to do something if you're not overwhelmed because, with pressure, people tend to fall back on routines - whether good or bad.

In a recent experiment, psychologist Wendy Wood, Ph.D., of the University of Southern California and one of the world's leading experts in habit formation, found that students fell into autopilot around the time of the test. If you get in the groove when relaxed, then when you are stressed, you are more likely to stay in the groove.

Tip #2: Identify why you don't want a new habit to grow.

People have mixed feelings about developing new behaviours, so be sure to consider what holds you back: time, commitment, motivation, a lack of immediate gratification, cash, and so on. You're not terrible at shifting mental barriers. You're just human.

Tip #3: Practice tolerance for irritation and delay gratification.

Research tells us that people who defer gratification for future happiness (instant pleasure) are better able to tolerate disappointment than those who catch short-term fixes. Stop doing something that is not healthy for you for a minute, or 10 minutes, or an hour, or until tomorrow.

Use thought incrementally. To soothe the disappointment with words of compassion and encouragement, say: I can do this, I'll be okay without my quick fix, and I'll love how I feel like making a healthy choice.

Tip #4: Highlight yourself and be proud of every little step you take to create a new habit.

It doesn't work to blame yourself. It only makes you feel bad and less likely to want to do good things. Reward yourself with generous congratulations when you make a positive choice and make you feel proud. It works better to feel proud than to be shameful.

Tip #5: Make sure you give yourself a new habit, but not to please others.

To make others happy or to stop being shamed by them, most people try to change. Make sure you're doing it for yourself and know why you're going to benefit from the change.

Changing habits is the most challenging thing we all face in our lives as no one is prepared to come out of their comfort zone and change their routine, setting priorities, leaving what you like for what is good for you. Habits are sometimes seen in the form of addictions. By following the above steps, you should be able to change your practices and your habits successfully; but changing or leaving cravings is not as easy as changing your habit to rise early. But it can be easy compared to abstaining from alcohol. Still, if you are motivated and consistent, you can manage to control yourself and leave your harmful habits. Leading a happy and healthy life should be your goal: improvement is life.

For further details: such as coaching and free downloadable
resources see our website here:
www.mindsetmastership.com

References

Anastacia. (n.d.). The Golden Loop of Habit Change. *https://www.bloomsandsmiles.com/the-golden-loop-of-habit-change/.*

Barnett, M. (n.d.). Good Habits, Bad Habits: A Conversation with Wendy Wood. *https://behavioralscientist.org/good-habits-bad-habits-a-conversation-with-wendy-wood/.*

Clear, J. (n.d.). The Ultimate Habit Tracker Guide: Why and How to Track Your Habits. *https://jamesclear.com/habit-tracker.*

Daniels, E. (n.d.). strategies to stay stick with your new habits. *https://learnevolveandthrive.com/how-to-make-good-habits-stick/.*

Edblad, P. (n.d.).
    https://patrikedblad.com/habits/how-to-change-your-habits.

Intrinsic Motivation. (n.d.). *https://psychology.iresearchnet.com/social-psychology/control/intrinsic-motivation/.*

K. (n.d.).
https://www.lifehack.org/797417/how-to-make-

changes-in-life. *How to Make Changes in Life To Be The Best Version of You.*

Logo, H. (n.d.). How to Change Habits and Start New Ones Using the Habit Loop. *https://habit.com/blog/2018/01/18/change-habits-start-new-ones-using-habit-loop/*

Maltz., M. (1960). Psycho-Cybernetics.

Parrish, R. (1992). Disrupting Habitual Patterns Through Meditation. Pp. https://mindworks.org/blog/overcoming-habitual-patterns-meditation/.

Pei-Ying Lin, W. W. (2015, November 9). Healthy eating habits protect against temptations. *https://dornsife.usc.edu/assets/sites/545/docs/lin.wood.mont erosso.2016.pdf.*

Petsinger, D. K. (n.d.). 6 Signs It's Time to Change Your Life. *https://www.lifehack.org/368124/6-signs-its-time-change-your-life.*

Stillman, J. (2016, July). This 1 Science-Backed Rule Is All You Need to Stay Motivated. pp. https://www.inc.com/jessica-stillman/follow-this-1-rule-to-maintain-peak-motivation.html.

Ryder, J. (2014, Jun 22,). https://www.psychologytoday.com/us/blog/hypno sis-the-power-trance/201406/hypnotic-regression-and-healing-the-unconscious-mind.